The Independent Reader

The Independent Reader

Skills for Building Comprehension and Vocabulary

Betty Sobel/Lorraine C. Smith

English Language Institute,
Queens College,
The City University of New York

Holt, Rinehart and Winston
New York   Chicago   San Francisco   Philadelphia
Montreal   Toronto   London   Sydney
Tokyo   Mexico City   Rio de Janeiro   Madrid

Photographs by Joseph Tenga.

Library of Congress Cataloging-in-Publication Data

Sobel, Betty.
    The independent reader.

    Includes index.
      1. College readers.   2. English language—Textbooks
for foreign speakers.   I. Smith, Lorraine C.   II. Title.
PE1122.S57   1986   428.6'4   85–17620
ISBN 0-03-001589-8

CBS COLLEGE PUBLISHING
Holt, Rinehart and Winston
The Dryden Press
Saunders College Publishing

Preface

This book is intended for intermediate to advanced ESL students for whom the reading selections provide a natural reading situation. That is, the vocabulary is not controlled, and the relative difficulty of the articles varies. Furthermore, the students are deliberately *not* primed with new vocabulary before reading an article, so that the reading experience will be comparable to picking up and reading a newspaper. The students need to understand that they will do more precise vocabulary work later on and that their primary goal is general comprehension.

Instructors can work on the articles in any order they choose because each chapter is an independent unit. The selections deal with aspects of American culture, areas of personal growth, and contemporary trends.

The aim of the book is to foster self-confidence and a positive attitude in students toward reading a text, magazine article, newspaper, or book in English as a result of the practical skills they will develop. These skills include determining the main idea of a reading passage, analyzing words, understanding the author's tone, and using grammatical clues to enhance comprehension. These skills encourage an interest in reading because reading becomes efficient: The thought flow of a text is maintained without lags in comprehension.

In each unit, students deal with new words in various contexts. They think about the words, define them, and apply them in speech and writing. The lessons promote a steady improvement in vocabulary and comprehension.

Acknowledgments

The authors appreciate the interest and efforts of those who participated in creating this text. The inspiration for this book came from our students through the years. They are always a challenge, and this book evolved after many semesters of work on effective materials for the students.

We wish to thank Anne Boynton-Trigg, our editor, whose expert vision expedited the arduous process of polishing the text. We would like to acknowledge the following reviewers of our manuscript for their constructive comments and their care in calling attention to small but important details: Lynette Black, Memphis State University; Robin Bosworth, Waubonsee Community College; Mary DeShazer, Xavier University; Vern Neal, Monterey Peninsula College; Mary Ellen Page, University of Florida; Grace Wylie, Florida Institute of Technology; Jean Zukowski/Faust, Northern Arizona University.

We wish also to thank Herbert Seliger, director of the English Language Institute (ELI) of Queens College of the City University of New York, who offered us invaluable guidance in the teaching concepts on which the book is based.

The faculty of the ELI often offered us advice, fresh ideas, moral support, and actual assistance toward the completion of the manuscript. Their encouragement and excitement were infectious, and for this we owe them a real debt of gratitude.

We wish to express our deep appreciation to our families and friends for their unwavering support, especially to Stanley, Henry, and Susan and to Peg, Cathy, and Winnie, who were proud and enthusiastic from Day One.

We are deeply indebted to Joseph Tenga, who had complete charge of the photography for the book. His fertile imagination and expertise in planning and executing the illustrations for the book have enhanced it immeasurably.

New York, N.Y.   BS
                                                                           LCS

Introduction to Instructors and Students

Each chapter in this book consists of the following:

—Introductory Questions
—Reading Passage
—A. True/False Statements
—B. Comprehension Questions
—C. Vocabulary in Context Exercise
—D. Detailed Comprehension Exercise
—E. Vocabulary in Context Quiz
—F. Topics for Discussion and Composition

There is an Answer Key at the end of the book.

Introductory Questions

The purpose of the introductory questions is to focus the students' attention on the subject matter of the passage and to motivate their interest. In a classroom situation, the time allotted for this exercise depends on the discussion raised by the students as well as on the instructor's preference.

The Reading Passage

Because the title is the author's first message about the passage, the students should think about it for a few minutes. Is the title a simple, clear statement about the passage? What is (are) the key word(s) in the title? Can you guess what the author will say about the topic?

After considering the title, the students will read the passage for the first time from beginning to end, without stopping to underline new words or look up their definitions. The students should try to read at a steady, unbroken rate. The aim of this first reading is to get a general understanding of the passage. After completing the first reading, the students will do the True/False exercise, which tests overall comprehension.

The next step is a second reading of the article. Ideally, the students try to read at a somewhat faster rate than the first time. After finishing the second reading, the students proceed to the Comprehension Questions. Because the Comprehension Questions deal with detailed information, the students may refer back to the reading passage for answers. In the classroom, the instructor may wish to review these questions before the second reading to help the students keep in mind the information they will be expected to draw from the passage. As with the first reading, the focus is on comprehension, not vocabulary.

The first of the Comprehension Questions is a multiple-choice question dealing with the main idea of the reading passage, that is, the statement that tells the reader what the entire passage is about. There will always be four choices, one of which is the correct answer. Each of the other three choices is incorrect for a specific reason, which will be one of the following:

1. The idea is too broad: It conveys more information than the story covers;
2. The idea is too narrow: It is only one detail in the passage, not the major idea;
3. The idea is not mentioned in the article.

In the classroom, the instructor checks the answers with the students and discusses the reasons for wrong and right answers. This procedure will clarify uncertainties and misunderstandings the students may have.

Vocabulary in Context Exercise

In each reading passage, some vocabulary items appear in boldface type. These words are the focus of the Vocabulary in Context Exercise. The purpose of this exercise is to train students to look at the *context* in which a word is found in order to understand its meaning. Figuring out the meaning of a word from its context reduces dependence on a dictionary, is less disruptive to the reading process, saves time, and is, therefore, a skill that promotes reading efficiency.

The exercise begins with a series of sentences or short passages in which the words in boldface type appear, again in boldface, in a different context. The students read the sentences carefully and try to understand the meaning of the boldface words. After they have studied the sentences, they read the definitions and synonyms that follow and match the words with their meanings.

This exercise is set up as a self-check. The students can go back after matching the words with their meanings and put the definitions or synonyms into the context of the sentences to see if they make sense. If they do, then the students have matched the words and meanings correctly. For example, in Chapter 1, in sentence 1 of Part A of the Vocabulary in Context Exercise, if the synonym *worried* or the synonym *apprehensive* is substituted for the word *anxious*, the sentence will make sense: *He had studied, but he still felt very worried.* Therefore, in Part B, *anxious* belongs in blank space number 5, along with the definition *worried; apprehensive.* All the synonyms of a word may not be familiar to the students, but this arrangement makes it simpler to learn the unknown words. The students can check their answers together in class or by referring to the Answer Key. When completed, this exercise serves as a useful vocabulary study guide.

Detailed Comprehension Exercise

The Detailed Comprehension Exercise trains the students to find and use all possible clues that lead to full comprehension of a reading passage. These clues may be structural or punctuation clues, key words that connect or contrast ideas, synonyms and explanations given in the passage itself, definitions that are hidden in one or more sentences, or a style of writing that leads to logical inferences and conclusions.

In this exercise, the students are asked to think about items from the passage that are indicated by line number. The students answer the specific questions that follow, and they can check their answers by referring to the Answer Key or through class discussion. Because the wording of individual answers will vary, the Answer Key can be used only as a guide here.

In order to do this exercise, the students must be familiar with such logical relationships as:

a. cause and effect
b. explanation and clarification
c. repetition and emphasis
d. example and illustration
e. contrast and opposition
f. similarities

In the classroom, the teacher may want to review grammatical and punctuation clues with the students when the need becomes evident.

Vocabulary in Context Quiz

The Vocabulary in Context Quiz is a recapitulation of the reading material with some words omitted. Because there are always several different and acceptable ways to express a thought or idea, any sensible or logical word in its proper form is considered a correct answer. Some blanks may require a different form of a previously used answer. However, an effort should be made to use the original words of the passage when filling in the blank spaces. The words in parentheses below the blank lines are synonyms of the omitted words and arc put there to be helpful. Proper word forms are very important. For example, note proper use of verb and adjective forms in the following:

a. John ____depends____ on his parents for support.
        (relies)

b. John ____depended____ on his parents for support last year.
        (relied)

c. John is ____dependent____ on his parents for support.
        (reliant)

This exercise will be timed by the instructor, or the students can time themselves. In this way, the students can measure their progress in working quickly and efficiently. Answers can be checked against the Answer Key. The instructor may also choose to use this exercise as a graded quiz.

When checking this exercise, the instructor will point out errors in usage and application of terms in order to clarify misunderstandings. In some cases, the instructor may find it useful to provide a list of word forms for the students to refer to. If the students want the forms of a new word (noun, verb, adjective, adverb), the instructor can provide them and the students can write them down.

Topics for Discussion and Composition

The Topics for Discussion and Composition may be used as points of departure for oral presentations or for written work. In either case, they provide the opportunity not only to use newly learned vocabulary but also to express personal opinions. The students are encouraged to apply the vocabulary presented and practiced in the chapter.

Contents

The Independent
Reader

The Misery
of Shyness

Introductory Questions

1. Many students find it difficult to start conversations with new classmates. What are some of the reasons for this difficulty?
2. Some people feel uncomfortable when others say nice things to them. For example, a friend may say, "That's a beautiful sweater you're wearing." Why would such a statement cause discomfort?
3. In college classes there are likely to be students who learn more quickly and more easily than you do. Does this mean you're a poor student? How do you feel whenever you understand that you are not the smartest student in the class?

The Misery of Shyness

Shyness is the cause of much unhappiness for a great many people. All kinds of people describe themselves as shy: short, tall, dull, intelligent, young, old, slim, overweight. Shy people are **anxious** and self-conscious; that is, they are excessively concerned with their own appearance and actions. Worrisome
5 thoughts are constantly swirling in their minds: What kind of impression am I making? Do they like me? Do I sound stupid? I'm ugly. I'm wearing unattractive clothes.

It is obvious that such uncomfortable feelings must affect people adversely. A person's self-concept is reflected in the way he or she behaves, and
10 the way a person behaves affects other people's reactions. In general, the way people think about themselves has a **profound** effect on all areas of their lives. For instance, people who have a positive sense of self-worth or high self-esteem usually act with confidence. Because they have self-assurance, they do not need constant **praise** and encouragement from others to feel good
15 about themselves. Self-confident people are their own best friends. They participate in life **enthusiastically** and **spontaneously.** They are not affected by what others think they "should" do. People with high self-esteem are not hurt by criticism; they do not regard criticism as personal rejection. Instead, they view criticism as suggestion for improvement.
20 In contrast, shy people, having low self-esteem, are likely to be passive and easily influenced by others. They need **reassurance** that they are doing "the right thing." Shy people are very sensitive to criticism; they feel it confirms their inferiority. They also find it difficult to be pleased by compliments because they believe they are unworthy of praise. A shy person may respond
25 to a compliment with a statement like this one: "You're just saying that to make me feel good. I know it's not true." It is clear that, while self-awareness is a healthy quality, overdoing it is detrimental, or harmful.

2

Can shyness be completely eliminated, or at least reduced? Fortunately, people can **overcome** shyness with determined and patient effort in building
30 self-confidence. Since shyness goes hand in hand with lack of self-esteem, it is important for people to accept their weaknesses as well as their strengths. For example, most people would like to be "A" students in every subject. It is not fair for them to label themselves inferior because they have difficulty in some areas. People's expectations of themselves must be realistic. **Dwelling**
35 **on** the impossible leads to a sense of inadequacy, and even feelings of envy, or jealousy. We are self-destructive when we envy a student who gets better grades.

If you are shy, here are some specific helpful steps toward building self-confidence and overcoming shyness:

40 1. Recognize your personal strengths and weaknesses. Everyone has both. As self-acceptance grows, shyness naturally diminishes.
2. Set reasonable goals. For example, you may be timid about being with a group of strangers at a party. Don't feel that you must converse with everyone. Concentrate on talking to only one or two people. You will feel
45 more comfortable.
3. Guilt and **shame** are destructive feelings. Don't waste time and energy on them. Suppose you have hurt someone's feelings. Feeling ashamed accomplishes nothing. Instead, accept the fact that you have made a mistake, and make up your mind to be more sensitive in the future.
50 4. There are numerous approaches to all issues. Few opinions are completely right or wrong. Don't be afraid to speak up and give your point of view.
5. Do not make negative comments about yourself. This is a form of self-rejection. Avoid describing yourself as stupid, ugly, **worthless,** a failure.
55 Accent the positive.
6. Accept criticism thoughtfully. Do not interpret it as a personal attack. If, for example, a friend complains about your cooking, accept it as a comment on your cooking, not yourself. Be assured that you are the same good friend; perhaps your cooking *could* improve.
60 7. Remember that everyone experiences some failures and disappointments. Profit from them as learning experiences. Very often a disappointment becomes a turning point for a wonderful experience to come along. For instance, you may be rejected by the college of your choice. However, at the college you actually attend, you may find a quality of education be-
65 yond what you had expected.
8. Do not associate with people who make you feel inadequate. Try to change their attitude or yours, or remove yourself from that relationship. People who hurt you do not have your best interests at heart.
9. Set aside time to relax, enjoy hobbies, and reevaluate your **goals** on a
70 regular basis. Time spent this way helps you learn more about yourself.
10. Practice being in social situations. Don't isolate yourself from people. Try making one acquaintance at a time; eventually you will circulate in large groups with skill and self-assurance.

Each one of us is a unique, worthwhile individual. We are interesting
75 in our own personal ways. The better we understand ourselves, the easier it
becomes to live up to our full **potential.** Let's not allow shyness to block our
chances for a rich and fulfilling life.

A. True/False Statements

After reading the passage for the first time, read the following statements and
check whether they are True (T) or False (F).

_____ T _____ F   1. All people who worry are shy.

_____ T _____ F   2. If we think well of ourselves, we will act with confi-
                       dence.

_____ T _____ F   3. People who are shy can't change.

_____ T _____ F   4. Shy people have trouble accepting compliments.

_____ T _____ F   5. We hurt ourselves when we have bad feelings toward a more intelligent student.

_____ T _____ F   6. Self-acceptance is an important step in overcoming shyness.

B. Comprehension Questions

1. The main idea of the article is:
   a. Shyness affects many people in our society.
   b. We can overcome shyness by talking to strangers.
   c. Shyness is caused by an unhappy childhood.
   d. Shyness causes unhappiness, but it can be overcome.
2. Why are shy people unhappy?
3. How do people with high self-esteem act? How do people with low self-esteem act?
4. How can people overcome shyness?
5. Is there a relationship, or connection, between self-acceptance and shyness?
6. Why is it so important to overcome shyness?

C. Vocabulary in Context Exercise: Part I

A. Read the sentences below carefully, and try to understand the meaning of the boldface words.
   1. John sat in the classroom and waited for the test to begin. He had studied, but he still felt very **anxious.** He needed to pass the test in order to graduate. When he read the test questions, he felt very relieved. He knew the answers! He would pass the test and graduate!
   2. Jill was always worrying about money. She was afraid that she wouldn't be able to pay her tuition. She spent hours thinking about how she would pay her rent and buy food. Her friends told her to stop **dwelling on** her money problems. They told her to get a job; then she wouldn't have to worry.
   3. Chris loved baseball. He listened **enthusiastically** to the local baseball games on the radio, and the scores of out-of-town games. He read the sports column every day, and he knew all the names of the teams and their members. He even bought baseball cards to trade with his friends.
   4. It took Tom a long time to **overcome** his fear of the dark. He had to

sleep with two lights on. Eventually, he could sleep with only one light on. Then he was able to sleep with a very small light on. Eventually, he was able to sleep without any lights on. He felt very proud of himself!

5. Ana is an intelligent person. She is also energetic, ambitious, and hardworking. Clearly, she has the **potential** to succeed in the new job that she is going to begin next week.

6. When Sam was a child, he saw a fireman run into a burning house and save a man's life. This experience had such a **profound** effect on Sam that he decided to become a fireman when he grew up.

7. While Mary was learning to cook, she always looked for **reassurance** from her mother that she was doing everything correctly. She said, "Mom, did I cook the steak too long? Mom, do you think the cake is done yet? Mom, does my soup taste good?"

B. Match the following words with the definitions and synonyms listed below.

anxious	enthusiastically	potential	reassurance
dwell on	overcome	profound	

1. _____ : possibility; capacity

2. _____ : get the better of; conquer

3. _____ : deep; not superficial

4. _____ : freedom from anxiety and fear

5. _____ : worried; apprehensive

6. _____ : think about at length; linger over

7. _____ : with feelings of excitement

C. Vocabulary in Context Exercise: Part II

A. Read the sentences below carefully, and try to understand the meaning of the boldface words.

1. Karen's grandfather asked her what she wanted her major to be in college. She said her **goal** was to get a degree in physics.

2. Children learn much more from **praise** than they learn from criticism. It's so much more positive to tell a child how well he did something than to point out what he did wrong.

3. Some students experience feelings of **shame** when an instructor asks them a question they cannot answer. They feel as though the entire class regards them as unintelligent, lazy people who didn't study. They think they have lost the instructor's respect.

4. I was sitting in the living room with my sister. We were both reading

books. Suddenly my sister looked up and said, "I have a great idea! Let's call up some friends and have a party! There's soda in the refrigerator, and we can buy some food from the store down the street." I agreed, and within an hour our house was full of friends eating, talking, and listening to music. I love these **spontaneous** parties.

5. I bought an old table at a house sale last month. It looked like a real antique, so I took it to an expert. Unfortunately, after he had examined it carefully, he told me it was **worthless.** I had paid fifty dollars for it, and he said I should never have bought it at all. I had thought it was worth two hundred dollars!

B. Match the following words with the definitions and synonyms listed below.

goal   shame   worthless
praise   spontaneous

1. _____ : commendation; speaking well of

2. _____ : without value

3. _____ : aim; purpose

4. _____ : impulsive; unpremeditated; not planned

5. _____ : a painful feeling caused by guilt or improper behavior

D. Detailed Comprehension Exercise

Answer the following questions. Refer back to the passage wherever necessary.

1. What is the relationship between these pairs of adjectives in lines 2–3: *short/tall; dull/intelligent; young/old; slim/overweight?*

   a. _____
   From the relationship, deduce the meanings of *dull* and *overweight.*

   b. **dull** means: _____

   c. **overweight** means: _____

2. "Shy people are anxious and self-conscious; *that is,* they are excessively concerned with their own appearance and actions." (lines 3–4)
   a. How does *that is,* connect what precedes it to what follows it?

   _____

   b. What does **self-conscious** mean? _____

   _____

3. "It is obvious that such uncomfortable feelings affect people adversely." (lines 8–9)
   Reread paragraph 1.
   a. What are the uncomfortable feelings to which this sentence refers? In other words, how do shy people feel?

   _____

   b. How do these feelings affect people? That is, do these feelings have a positive effect or a negative effect on shy people?

   _____

   c. From what you have decided about the effect of *such uncomfortable feelings*, what does **adversely** mean? _____

4. "For instance, people who have a positive sense of self-worth, or high self-esteem, usually act with confidence." (lines 12–13)
   a. How does *for instance,* connect this sentence with the sentence before

   it? _____
   b. In this sentence, what word is a synonym of **self-worth?**

   _____

   c. What grammatical clue in this sentence gave you this information?

   _____

5. "Because they have self-assurance, they do not need constant praise and encouragement from others to feel good about themselves." (lines 13–15)
   How does this sentence relate to the previous sentence?

   _____

6. "They are not affected by what others think they 'should' do." (lines 16–17)
   a. Why is *should* in quotation marks? In other words, what message is

   the author trying to convey to the reader? _____

   _____

7. "Instead, they view criticism as suggestion for improvement." (lines 18–19)
   Instead is a clue to the relationship between lines 18 and 19. What is the

   relationship? _____

8. Paragraph 3 begins with the words *In contrast.* How do these words show the relationship between paragraphs 2 and 3?

   _____

   _____

9. "They need reassurance that they are doing 'the right thing.'" (lines 21–22)

Why is *the right thing* in quotation marks? In other words, what does the author imply by using quotation marks?

_____

_____

10. "It is clear that, while self-awareness is a healthy quality, overdoing it is detrimental, or harmful." (lines 26–27)
   a. In this sentence, *while* does *not* indicate a period of time. What purpose does it serve in this sentence?

   _____

   b. Look at the word *overdoing*. It is composed of two parts. Based on the meanings of these two parts, what does **overdo** mean?

   _____

   c. What is a synonym of **detrimental?** _____
   d. How do you know this word is a synonym of *detrimental?*

   _____

11. "Can shyness be completely eliminated, or at least reduced?" (line 28) How does this sentence clarify the meanings of **eliminated** and **reduced?** The clue here is in the use of *or at least.*

   a. What does **eliminate** mean? _____

   b. What does **reduce** mean? _____
12. "Since shyness goes hand in hand with lack of self-esteem, it is important to accept our weaknesses as well as our strengths." (lines 30–31)
   a. How does the first part of this sentence relate to the second part

   logically? _____

   _____

   b. What does **since** mean in this sentence? _____
13. ". . . feelings of envy, or jealousy. We are self-destructive when we envy a student who gets better grades." (lines 35–37)

   a. What is a synonym of **envy?** _____

   b. How do lines 36–37 tie in with feelings of envy? _____

   _____

14. "As self-acceptance grows, shyness naturally diminishes." (line 41)
   a. What is the logical relationship between the two parts of this

   sentence? _____

   b. According to this logic, what does **diminish** mean? _____

15. ". . . perhaps your cooking *could* improve." (line 59)

   Why is *could* underlined? _____

16. "Very often a disappointment becomes a turning point for a wonderful experience to come along." (lines 61–62)
   a. Read lines 62–65. What is this anecdote an example of?

   _____

   b. What was the turning point? _____

   _____

17. "Practice being in social situations. Don't isolate yourself from people." (line 71)

   a. What does **isolate** mean? _____

E. Vocabulary in Context Quiz

Complete each blank space with a synonym of the word(s) in parentheses. You may need to use more than one word.

   Young, old, slim, (1) _____, male, female: all kinds of
                              (fat)
people are shy. They are (2) _____ concerned with their
                                (overly)
appearance and behavior. They become (3) _____ about
                                            (apprehensive)
the impression they make on others. They (4) _____
                                                (do to excess)
by (5) _____ their own behavior, always rating it
          (lingering over)
(6) _____. They let themselves be influenced by others
      (negatively)
because they believe their own ideas are (7) _____.
                                              (without value)
   People with a positive self-image act with confidence. They don't

require (8) _____ from others to respect themselves. It is a
              (commendation)
fact that everyone has both weaknesses and strengths. Secure people do not

ignore their strengths; they try to live up to their (9) _____.
                                                          (capabilities)
Their behavior is (10) _____, and they are not disturbed by
                          (impulsive)
criticism.

Shyness does not have to be a permanent condition; it can be (11) _____ by anyone who makes a serious decision to
    (conquered)
do so. The following are helpful suggestions for (12) _____
                                                    (reducing)
shyness.

Study your good qualities and your weaknesses. Make the most of your assets, or good points, and work on getting rid of the weaknesses gradually. For (13) _____, if you are shy with strangers at a party, make
        (example)
it your (14) _____ to speak with only one or two people. This
        (aim)
much is manageable. At times when you hurt someone's feelings, don't concentrate on that (15) _____ . Apologize if you wish. Be
                        (too much)
more sensitive in the future.

Look upon disappointments as learning experiences, and profit from them. Associate with people you respect, and avoid those who make you feel inadequate. They are not friends, and are (16) _____ to your
                                                    (harmful)
well-being. Don't (17) _____ yourself from people. Make
                        (separate)
acquaintances one at a time. Success will (18) _____ your
                                                (lessen)
fears and build (19) _____ .
                    (self-confidence)
Your opinion of yourself has a(n) (20) _____ effect on
                                        (deep)
your life. Don't allow insecurity and (21) _____ to cause you
                                            (jealousy)
unhappiness. Express yourself confidently and (22) _____ ,
                                                    (with excitement)
(23) _____ your thoughts are as valuable as anyone
        (because)
else's. (24) _____ shyness, build up your feelings of
            (Get rid of)
(25) _____ , and live a richer life.
        (self-worth)

F. Topics for Discussion and Composition

1. Of the ten steps given to overcome shyness, discuss the three most valuable in your opinion.
2. How would you identifiy your strengths and weaknesses?
3. How would you help a good friend deal with his or her shyness?
4. How do you think people become shy?
5. "Self-confident people are their own best friends." In what ways is this statement true?

Making a Cultural Change

Introductory Questions

1. Many students want to study in a foreign country. Why do you think they choose to do this?
2. On the other hand, many students don't want to study in a foreign country, but they go nevertheless. Why do you think they do so?
3. Do you think the adjustment to a new country would be more easily made alone, or if one's whole family came along? Why?
4. Is it realistic to expect to be comfortable immediately after arriving in a new country? Why? Why not?

Making a Cultural Change

Until a relatively short time ago, traveling abroad was limited to well-to-do tourists and **prosperous** businesspeople. Flying abroad was atypical for the average person. In time, however, plane travel became safer, more convenient, and less expensive. As a result, people of **diverse** backgrounds now fly
5 to distant places for pleasure, business, or education. Very often government officials and business representatives fly to one country for a breakfast or lunch conference, then fly to another country for a dinner meeting.

With the world becoming smaller, many young adults make the decision to study in foreign universities. In fact, the United States is host to thousands
10 of foreign students. It is an exciting, **challenging** experience to live in a foreign country. Anyone who can study abroad is fortunate; but, of course, it is not easy to make the transition from one culture to another. One faces many **hurdles.**

The student leaves behind a familiar, comfortable, loving **environment.**
15 Back home, he[1] has his family, friends, and acquaintances. He knows the language, politics, currency, food, social customs, and so forth. He has internalized all the intangible aspects of his native culture, such as body language, bargaining practices, and efforts to minimize waste via recycling, etc. In short, he knows "the system." Then one day he leaves all this behind and
20 suddenly finds himself in a place where everyone and everything is strange, perhaps even **perplexing.** All this strangeness is a major **jolt** to a person's self-assurance. This abrupt change often leads to a reaction called culture shock.

Foreigners experience varying degrees of culture shock. The symptoms

---

[1]Throughout the text an attempt has been made to achieve a balance between masculine and feminine gender-specific pronouns. "She/her" is thus used in place of the generic "he/his" (see lines 32–34 following), and the two may alternate within a single passage, as here. Such alternation avoids overuse of the sometimes awkward "he or she / his or her" pronoun sequence.

14

range from being ill-at-ease to being seriously depressed. Feeling homesick,
25 irritable, unhappy, and very sensitive are other signs of culture shock. It is
easy to understand that the endless frustrations of the early days in a new
country would **generate** discontent, discomfort, and perhaps **hostility.** People
are always at ease in a familiar environment. A **mature,** realistic person experiences mild, temporary symptoms; the insecure newcomer suffers from a
30 more serious case of culture shock.

During the inevitable period of adjustment, the international student
tends to complain about everything in the host country. In fact, she[2] is likely
to **exaggerate** the problems. When she **encounters** another miserable com-
patriot, she has a real outlet for unhappy feelings. Together they can **gripe** in
35 their native language. Although this complaining provides temporary satisfaction, it certainly does not facilitate adapting to a new society. Being negative
will never **alleviate** the feelings of frustrations. The mature person under-
stands that a positive attitude, determination, and **flexibility** are crucial in
making the transition successful. A sense of humor is a big help.
40 The following suggestions have been found to be helpful in **combating**
culture shock.

1. Keep busy. Get to know the area where you live by strolling around and
   observing. Become familiar with the stores in the neighborhood and the
   kinds of merchandise sold. Locate the post office, library, schools, hospital,
45   and supermarkets. Say hello to a neighbor in your building, and perhaps
   start a friendship.
2. Become friendly with classmates. Spend some out-of-school time together.
3. Do something you enjoy. Phone your family back home. Write a letter to
   a friend. Contact a relative or acquaintance whose address you may have.
50   **Browse** through department stores. Visit a museum. Walk through a new
   area of town. See a play. Go to a movie.
4. Forget that your English is less than perfect, and feel free to ask people
   for information, guidance, or directions. Many people are friendly, sympathetic, and helpful. It is important not to dwell on negative incidents.
55   Disappointments are simply a fact of life.
5. Be **flexible.** Laugh at the errors you make; they are usually not serious.
   Make up your mind that you are going to enjoy your new adventure.

With the right attitude, living in a foreign country can be a priceless,
enriching period in a person's life. It is a form of education—an exciting form.
60 The above recommendations will help a person **cope with** life abroad.

---

[2]Note use of "generic *she*" in this paragraph. See footnote 1 above.

A. True/False Statements

After reading the passage for the first time, read the following statements and check whether they are True (T) or False (F).

_____ T _____ F 1. It is always easy to cope with life in a different culture.

_____ T _____ F 2. Culture shock affects all foreigners in the same way.

_____ T _____ F 3. In order to make a successful transition from one culture to another, a positive attitude and some effort are very important.

_____ T _____ F 4. According to the author, phoning family and writing to friends will make international students even more homesick.

_____ T _____ F 5. Being able to adapt to new situations will help lessen feelings of culture shock.

B. Comprehension Questions

1. The main idea of the article is:
   a. Culture shock can be overcome by getting to know your neighborhood very well.
   b. Many international students are affected by culture shock, but it can be overcome.
   c. Many international students who experience culture shock don't like foreign food and lose weight.
   d. Culture shock is an unpleasant emotional experience from which many people suffer.
2. Why do many young people go to foreign countries?
3. What are some of the cultural changes that must be made?
4. What is culture shock?
5. What are some of the signs of culture shock?
6. How can culture shock be overcome?

C. Vocabulary in Context Exercise: Part I

A. Read the sentences below carefully, and try to understand the meaning of the boldface words.
   1. Mary had a very bad headache. She took two aspirin and lay down for a while. The aspirin and the rest helped **alleviate** her headache, and she went back to work feeling much better.
   2. I like to go into department stores and **browse.** I never buy anything, but I enjoy seeing the latest fashions and looking at the new furniture.
   3. Racing car drivers find the yearly 500-mile race **challenging.** The competing drivers are brave and skilled, and the route is difficult and dangerous. They may win the race, or they may be hurt or even killed. It's all part of the race!
   4. The little girl tried to **combat** her fear of dogs by walking up to her friend's dog and touching it gently. When she did, she felt less afraid.
   5. Susan is very quiet and shy. She finds it very difficult to **cope with** meeting new people. For that reason, she does not like to go to new places or to parties, and she does not go out very often.
   6. The students in most ESL classes are from **diverse** countries. For example, in one class there may be people from Japan, Greece, Korea, Colombia, China, France, and Thailand.
   7. When Joe walks around his neighborhood, he sometimes **encounters** a friend he hasn't seen in a long time. He usually invites his friend for a cup of coffee.
   8. A fish's natural **environment** is water, with rocks or plants to give it protection from bigger fish. When it is removed from this environment, it dies.
   9. Tom won $5,000 in the lottery. He ran home and said to his wife, "We're rich! We won more money than we can ever spend! Let's buy a new car!" His wife said, "Don't **exaggerate.** Tell me how much money you really won."

10. I'd like to go out to dinner to an Indian restaurant, but I'm **flexible.**
     If you prefer a French or a Chinese restaurant, we can have Indian
     food next week instead of tonight.
B. Match the following words with the definitions and synonyms listed
   below.

alleviate	challenging	cope with	encounter	exaggerate
browse	combat	diverse	environment	flexible (adj.)
				flexibility (n.)

1. _____ : stimulating; exciting, but difficult to do

2. _____ : able to adapt or change

3. _____ : meet; find

4. _____ : relieve; lessen

5. _____ : surroundings

6. _____ : look around casually

7. _____ : overstate the truth

8. _____ : varied; differing

9. _____ : manage; deal with

10. _____ : fight

C. Vocabulary in Context Exercise: Part II

A. Read the sentences below carefully, and try to understand the meaning of
   the boldface words.
   1. The city built a new power plant in order to **generate** more electricity
      for the needs of the people.
   2. You are always **griping** that I don't cook delicious food. Instead of
      always grumbling about it, why don't you cook for yourself?
   3. My dog is **hostile** to strangers. Therefore, until he gets to know you,
      he will bark at you and may even try to bite you.
   4. John wanted a car, but there were many **hurdles** he had to overcome.
      First, he had to get a job and save his money. Then he had to take
      driving lessons. After that he had to pass the driving test. Finally, he
      had to shop for a car and get a car loan from the bank.
   5. If you put your finger into an electrical outlet, you will receive a very
      unpleasant **jolt.**
   6. Even though Maria is only 17 years old, she is quite **mature.** She
      handles situations in a very adult way, and she does not behave child-
      ishly any longer. All in all, she's a very responsible individual.

7. When you begin to study chemistry, the symbols may be very **perplexing** to you at first, and you will not understand what they mean. After studying for a while, however, you will know them very well.
8. My friend is a very **prosperous** businessman. In fact, he opened three new stores last year and plans to open five more new stores this year.
9. In New York City, the temperature may **range** from 95 degrees in the summer to 10 degrees in the winter.
10. Harry would like to get up early every day. Nevertheless, he **tends to** turn off his alarm clock and go back to sleep. As a result, he gets up early only once or twice a week.

B. Match the following words with the definitions and synonyms listed below.

generate	hostile (adj.)	jolt	perplexing	range
gripe	hostility (n.)	mature	prosperous	tend to
	hurdle			

1. _____ : shock

2. _____ : produce

3. _____ : fully developed mentally and emotionally

4. _____ : successful; thriving

5. _____ : complain

6. _____ : be inclined to

7. _____ : confusing; puzzling

8. _____ : change or differ within limits

9. _____ : obstacle; barrier

10. _____ : unfriendly; not hospitable

D. Detailed Comprehension

Answer the following questions. Refer back to the passage wherever necessary.

1. ". . . traveling abroad was limited to well-to-do tourists and prosperous businesspeople. Flying abroad was atypical for the average person." (lines 1–3)

   a. What does **well-to-do** mean? _____

   b. How do you know? _____

   c. What does **atypical** mean? _____

d. How do you know? _____

2. "With the world becoming smaller. . . . " (line 8)

   a. Is the world really becoming smaller? _____

   b. What impression, or picture, is the author trying to give the reader?

   _____

3. " . . . the United States is host to thousands of foreign students." (lines
   9–10)

   What does **host** mean? _____

   _____

4. " . . . it is not easy to make the transition from one culture to another."
   (lines 11–12)

   a. What does **transition** mean? _____

   b. How do *from* and *to* relate to the word *transition*? _____

   _____

5. "One faces many hurdles." (lines 12–13)
   What does **faces** mean?

   _____

6. "In short, he knows 'the system.' " (lines 18–19)

   a. What does **in short** mean? _____

   b. How does *in short* relate lines 15–18 to *he knows "the system"*? _____

   _____

   c. What does **the system** mean? _____

   _____

7. "The symptoms range from being ill-at-ease to being seriously depressed.
   Feeling homesick, irritable, unhappy, and very sensitive are other signs
   of culture shock." (lines 23–25)

   a. In these lines, which word is a synonym of **symptom**? _____

   b. How do you know? _____

8. "People are always at ease in a familiar environment." (lines 27–28)
   Compare *at ease* here with *ill-at-ease* in line 24.

   a. What does **at ease** mean? _____

   b. What does **ill-at-ease** mean? _____

   c. How are the two terms related? _____

9. " . . . the insecure newcomer suffers from a more serious case of culture shock. (lines 29 – 30)
Analyze the word **newcomer**. What meaning can you get from looking at

the three parts of this word? _____

_____

10. "Together they can gripe in their native language. Although this complaining provides temporary satisfaction, . . . " (lines 34 – 36)

What does *this complaining* refer to? _____

11. "Get to know the area where you live by strolling around and observing." (lines 42 – 43)
From the sense of this sentence, what do you think **strolling around**

means? _____

12. "It is important not to dwell on negative incidents. Disappointments are simply a fact of life." (lines 54 – 55)

What is **a fact of life?** _____

13. "With the right attitude, living in a foreign country can be a priceless, enriching period in a person's life." (lines 58 – 59)
Look at the word **priceless.** It means "without price," but what is the value of something priceless? In other words, if something is *priceless*,

what is its worth? _____

14. "It is a form of education—an exciting form." (line 59)
How does the dash relate what follows it to what precedes it?

_____

15. "The above recommendations will help you cope with life abroad." (line 60)

What does **abroad** mean? _____

E. Vocabulary in Context Quiz

Complete each blank space with a synonym of the word(s) in parentheses. You may need to use more than one word.

Airports are busy with businesspeople and tourists going to faraway

places all over the world. Years ago, it was (1) _____
(unusual)
for the average person to take a trip by plane. Today, many people of

(2) _____ backgrounds fly to distant places on a regular basis.
(differing)

Thousands of young adults choose the (3) _____ experience
 (stimulating)
of getting an education in a foreign country. For students, it is an exciting

opportunity, but it also means facing many (4) _____. There
 (obstacles)
is a complete change in (5) _____; the student goes from
 (surroundings)
the familiar and comfortable to the strange and (6) _____.
 (puzzling)
This (7) _____ to one's self-assurance is called culture
 (shock)
shock, and it is felt in varying degrees. (8) _____
 (Signs)
range from mild to serious. They include feeling homesick, irritable,

unhappy, and even (9) _____. A realistic, well-prepared,
 (unfriendly)
(10) _____ student experiences the milder symptoms.
 (emotionally developed)
   In the early period of adjustment, the foreign student faces many

problems. She (11) _____   (12) _____
 (is inclined to)   (overstate)
them in her own mind. If, however, she (13) _____
 (meets)
someone from her native country and (14) _____ about
 (complains)
her frustrations, this complaining releases some tension. A negative

attitude does not help (15) _____ problems. A positive atti-
 (relieve)
tude, (16) _____, determination, and a sense of humor are
 (adaptability)
qualities that make it easier to (17) _____ in a foreign culture.
 (manage)
   The   following   recommendations   are   helpful   in

(18) _____ the stresses of culture shock:
 (fighting)

1. Become familiar with your neighborhood.
2. Be friendly to classmates, and share some after-school activities with them.
3. Do something that gives you pleasure as often as you can. For example,

(19) _____ through famous; interesting areas and museums.
 (look casually)

Expect most people to be friendly and sympathetic, although there may be a few who show hostility.

The   experience   of   living   in   a   foreign   country   is (20) _____.
    (invaluable)

F. Topics for Discussion and Composition

1. What cultural changes have you had to make in coming to the United States?
2. What cultural changes have you found most difficult to make?
3. Have you experienced culture shock? How did you feel?
4. What have you found helpful in overcoming culture shock?

Latchkey Children— Knock, Knock, Is Anybody Home?

Introductory Questions

1. What are some reasons that mothers of young children might have for taking full-time jobs?
2. In your country, what arrangements do working parents make for the care of their children after school?
3. How do you think parents might feel if they had to leave their children unsupervised for several hours each day? How do you think children might feel about being left alone for several hours each day?

Latchkey Children—Knock, Knock, Is Anybody Home?

In the United States the cost of living has been steadily rising for the past few decades. Food prices, clothing costs, housing expenses, and tuition **fees** are constantly getting higher and higher. Partly because of financial need, and partly because of career choices for personal **fulfillment,** mothers have been
5 leaving the traditional role of full-time homemaker. Increasingly they have been taking **salaried** jobs outside the home.

Making such a **significant** role change affects the entire family, especially the children. Some **consequences** are obvious. For example, dinnertime is at a later hour. The emotional impact, on the other hand, can be more subtle.
10 Mothers leave home in the morning, feeling guilty because they will not be home when their children return from school. They **suppress** their guilt since they believe that their working will **benefit** everyone in the long run. The income will enable the family to save for college tuition, take an extended vacation, buy a new car, and so on.
15 The emotional impact on the children can be significant. It is quite common for children to feel hurt and resentful. After all, they are alone several hours, and they feel that their mothers should "be there" for them. They might need assistance with their homework or want to share the day's activities. All too often, however, the mothers arrive home exhausted and face the
20 immediate task of preparing dinner. Their priority is making the evening meal for the family, not engaging in relaxed conversation.

Latchkey children range in age from six to thirteen. On a daily basis they return from school and unlock the door to their home with the key hanging around their necks. They are now on their own, alone, in quiet, empty
25 rooms. For some youngsters, it is a productive period of private time, while for others it is a frightening, lonely **void.** For reasons of safety, many parents forbid their children to go out to play or to have visitors at home. The youngsters, therefore, feel isolated.

25

Latchkey children who were interviewed reported diverse reactions.
30 Some latchkey children said that being on their own for a few hours each day
fostered, or stimulated, a sense of independence and responsibility. They felt
loved and trusted, and this feeling encouraged them to be self-confident.
Latchkey girls, by observing how their mothers coped with the demands of a
family and a job, learned the role model of a working mother. Some children
35 stated that they used their **unsupervised** free time to perfect their athletic
skills, such as playing basketball. Others read books or practiced a musical
instrument. These children looked upon their free time after school as an
opportunity for personal development. It led to positive, productive, and valuable experiences.
40   Conversely, many latchkey children expressed much bitterness, resentment, and anger for being made to live in this fashion. Many claimed that too
much responsibility was placed on them at an early age; it was an overwhelming **burden.** They were little people who really wanted to be protected, encouraged, and cared for through attention from their mothers. Coming home
45 to an empty house was disappointing, lonely, and often frightening. They felt
abandoned by their mothers. After all, it seemed to them that most other

children had "normal" families whose mothers were "around," whereas their own mothers were never home. Many children turned on the television for the whole afternoon day after day, in order to diminish feelings of isolation;
50 furthermore, the voices were comforting. Frequently, they would **doze off.**

Because of either economic necessity or strong determination for personal **fulfillment,** or both, the **phenomenon** of latchkey children is widespread in our society. Whatever the reason, it is a compelling situation with which families must cope. The question to ask is not whether or not mothers should
55 work full-time. Given the reality of the situation, the question to ask is: how can an **optimum** plan be worked out to deal effectively with the situation?

It is advisable for all members of the family to express their feelings and concerns about the **inevitable** changes **candidly.** These remarks should be discussed fully. Many factors must be taken into consideration: the children's
60 personality and maturity, the amount of time the children will be alone, the safety of the neighborhood, accessibility of help in case of an emergency. Of supreme importance is the quality of the relationship between parents and children. It is most important that children be secure in the knowledge that they are loved. Feeling loved provides invaluable emotional strength to cope
65 successfully with almost any difficulty that arises in life.

A. True/False Statements

After reading the passage for the first time, read the following statements and check whether they are True (T) or False (F).

_____ T _____ F   1. All women work full-time because of financial necessity.

_____ T _____ F   2. When mothers begin to work full-time, life goes on as usual at home.

_____ T _____ F   3. Full-time working mothers do not give up their household responsibilities.

_____ T _____ F   4. Not all the effects of this arrangement are obvious or clear.

_____ T _____ F   5. It is important for family members to cooperate in order for this arrangement to work smoothly.

B. Comprehension Questions

1. The main idea of the article is:
   a. Because the latchkey-child arrangement has negative as well as positive aspects, families must discuss and plan very carefully.
   b. Many school children return to empty homes because their mothers work, and these children are called "latchkey children."

c. Some children love being home alone and find things to do, but other children hate being home alone.

d. Children receive many new toys and games from their mothers when they work full-time.

2. What are some reasons for mothers to take on full-time jobs?

3. Discuss some of the effects on a child of living in a family with a working mother.

4. Define a latchkey child.

5. What factors should families consider when making arrangements for latch-key children?

C. Vocabulary in Context Exercise: Part I

A. Read the sentences below carefully, and try to understand the meaning of the boldface words.

1. A program of regular exercise has many **benefits.** First, it increases the air capacity of the lungs. Second, it strengthens the heart. Third, it increases the body's ability to work longer without tiring. Fourth, it improves mental health.

2. As a boy, Joseph had to go to work when his father died. He was responsible for his sick mother and his four younger brothers and sisters. At the age of twelve, he had two full-time jobs in addition to being responsible for fixing the house. It was a terrible **burden** for a boy so young.

3. When Sara refused to marry Dennis, he asked her why. She wanted to speak **candidly,** but she was afraid of hurting his feelings, so she avoided telling him the truth.

4. The high salary, prestige, and opportunity for advancement were **compelling** reasons for taking the job.

5. Harry was constantly absent from his classes, and he never studied for any tests. The **consequences** were not surprising. At the end of the term he failed all his courses, and he was thrown out of school.

6. Susan was so tired when she came home that she lay on the couch and **dozed off** for half an hour. When she woke up, she felt much better.

7. When Tom went away to college, he had to pay a registration **fee,** fees for room and board, and a parking permit fee, in addition to his tuition.

8. Many people find **fulfillment** when they successfully complete a task they have worked hard to do.

B. Match the following words with the definitions and synonyms listed below.

| benefit | candidly | consequence | fee |
| burden | compelling | doze off | fulfillment |

1. _____ : a fixed charge

2. _____ : good; advantage

3. _____ : satisfaction; completion

4. _____ : result; effect

5. _____ : weight; load

6. _____ : strongly convincing

7. _____ : fall into a light sleep

8. _____ : openly; plainly

C. Vocabulary in Context Exercise: Part II

A. Read the sentences below carefully, and try to understand the meaning of the boldface words.
   1. If you continually drive through red lights, speed on the highway, and park in illegal spots, it is **inevitable** that you will get a ticket.
   2. This plant will grow tall and bushy under **optimum** conditions, i.e., plenty of sunlight, adequate water, and regular feeding with plant food. However, if your apartment isn't sunny, the plant will remain small.
   3. A solar eclipse, when the earth, the moon, and the sun are in a direct line, is an exciting **phenomenon** that people look forward to observing when it occurs.
   4. Unlike **salaried** jobs, for which workers receive regular wages, volunteer jobs are unpaid.
   5. The Fourth of July is a **significant** date in American history. It is the day the Declaration of Independence was signed.
   6. In countries where freedom of speech is a guaranteed right, the government cannot **suppress** the newspapers. They are not under government control and cannot be prevented from printing the truth.
   7. Many people are hard workers and do their jobs well even when they are **unsupervised,** whereas others are lazy and work only when their employers are watching over them.
   8. Phil's wife was his constant companion. They spent all their time together and did everything together. When she died suddenly, he was left with a tremendous **void** in his life. He had no friends to help him occupy his time and keep him company.
B. Match the following words with the definitions and synonyms listed below.

inevitable	phenomenon (sing.)	significant	unsupervised
optimum	phenomena (pl.)	suppress	void
	salaried		

   1. _____ : a fact or event of special interest

   2. _____ : important; notable

3. _____ : an empty space; a gap

4. _____ : unavoidable; certain to occur

5. _____ : not under constant observation

6. _____ : most favorable; best possible under the circumstances

7. _____ : crush; put down

8. _____ : paid

D. Detailed Comprehension Exercise

Answer the following questions. Refer back to the passage wherever necessary.

1. "Food prices, clothing costs, housing expenses, and tuition fees are constantly getting higher and higher." (lines 2–3)
Look at the words *prices, costs, expenses,* and *fees*. What do they all refer

to? _____

2. "Making such a significant role change affects the entire family." (line 7)
What is the role change referred to in this sentence?

_____

3. "Some consequences are obvious. For example, dinnertime is at a later
hour. The emotional impact, on the other hand, can be more subtle."
(lines 8–9)
a. What is an obvious consequence of the mother's role change?

_____

b. What is a subtle consequence of the mother's role change?

_____

c. What is the difference between *subtle* and *obvious?*

_____

d. How does *on the other hand* relate what follows it to what precedes

it? _____

e. What does **on the other hand** mean? _____

4. "They suppress their guilt since they believe that their working will benefit everyone in the long run. The income will enable the family to save
for college tuition, take an extended vacation, buy a new car, and so on."
(lines 11–14)

a. How does the first sentence relate to the second sentence?

_____

b. What does **benefit** mean? _____

5. "It is quite common for children to feel hurt and resentful. After all, they are alone several hours, and they feel that their mothers should 'be there' for them." (lines 15–17)

a. How does *after all* relate what follows it to the preceding sentence?

_____

b. Why is *"be there"* in quotation marks? _____

_____

6. "They might need assistance with their homework or want to share the day's activities. All too often, however, the mothers arrive home exhausted and face the immediate task of preparing dinner. Their priority is making the evening meal for the family, not engaging in relaxed conversation." (lines 17–21)

a. How does *"all too often, however . . ."* relate what follows it to what

precedes it? _____

b. What does **priority** mean? _____

7. "Latchkey children range in age from six to thirteen." (line 22)

How old are latchkey children? That is, what does **range** mean?

_____

8. ". . . they return from school and unlock the door. . . . They are now on their own, alone, in quiet, empty rooms." (lines 23–25)

What does **on their own** mean? _____

9. "Some latchkey children said that being on their own for a few hours each day fostered, or stimulated, a sense of independence. . . . " (lines 30–31)

a. What does **fostered** mean? _____

b. How do you know? _____

10. Read paragraph 5, then read paragraph 6. How does the word *conversely* in line 40 relate these two paragraphs?

_____

11. "Coming home to an empty house was disappointing, lonely, and often frightening. They felt abandoned by their mothers. After all, it seemed to them that most other children had 'normal' families whose mothers were 'around,' whereas their own mothers were never home." (lines 44–48)

a. What does **abandoned** mean? _____

b. How do you know? _____

c. According to the unhappy latchkey children, what is a **normal** family? _____

d. Why does the author put *around* in quotation marks? What does **around** mean in this context? _____
_____

e. How does *whereas* connect what precedes it to what follows it?
_____

12. "Many children turned on the television for the whole afternoon day after day, in order to diminish feelings of isolation; furthermore, the voices were comforting." (48–50)
How does *furthermore* connect what follows it to what precedes it?

13. ". . . the phenomenon of latchkey children is widespread in our society." (lines 52–53)
The word *widespread* consists of two parts. Look at the two parts. What does **widespread** mean? _____
_____

14. ". . . . the phenomenon of latchkey children is widespread in our society. . . . Given the reality of the situation, the question to ask is. . . . " (lines 52–55)

What does **given the reality of the situation** mean? _____

15. "Many factors must be taken into consideration: the children's personality and maturity, the amount of time the children will be alone, the safety of the neighborhood, accessibility of help in case of an emergency." (lines 59–61)

a. What does the colon after the word *consideration* do?
_____

b. What does **accessibility** mean? _____

c. How do you know? _____

E. Vocabulary in Context Quiz

Complete each blank space with a synonym of the word(s) in parentheses. You may need to use more than one word.

Year after year, ever-increasing numbers of mothers of school-age children are giving up the traditional role of full-time homemaker. They don't stay home a full day; they go to work. Cost-of-living expenses are (1)_____ getting higher. As a result, many mothers are
(steadily)
(2) _____ to get (3) _____ jobs. In other in-
(forced)   (paid)
stances, mothers look for personal (4) _____ through full-time
(satisfaction)
employment.

When a mother works, there are many (5) _____. Some
(effects)
are obvious; others are (6) _____. They range from a change
(hard to describe)
in conversation topics at dinnertime to feelings of (7) _____
(anger)
on the part of some children. Working mothers frequently have guilt feelings for not being home to (8) _____ their children. They
(observe)
(9) _____ their guilt by thinking of all the
(crush)
(10) _____ their income makes possible.
(advantages)

Latchkey children return from school daily to an empty home. Results of interviews with these children showed (11) _____ reactions
(a variety of)
to this lifestyle. For some youngsters being alone was a great
(12) _____ to enjoy free time in their own way. They said that
(chance)
they became more self-confident and independent. In addition to doing their homework, they worked on such hobbies as stamp collecting. Others
(13) _____ their athletic skills, such as playing handball.
(improved)
(14)_____ , other latchkey children found their home a
(On the other hand)
distressing, lonely (15) _____ . They were disappointed and
(empty space)
(16) _____ about being left alone. Many mothers
(angry)
(17) _____ their children to leave the house or have playmates
(do not permit)

visit. This restriction brought on feelings of isolation in some youngsters. They regarded being left alone as a(n) (18) _____. They
(weight)
needed attention, protection, and care, and they felt deprived for not getting it. With nobody home every afternoon, many children were frightened, and used TV as a "companion." Frequently they would (19) _____.
(fall asleep)

When mothers get full-time jobs, they must make (20) _____ plans for their children to cope with being alone.
(the best possible)
Everyone must be (21) _____ in airing his or her concerns
(open)
and fears. Reliable sources of (22) _____ must be available in
(help)
case of emergencies. The personality and interests of the children must be carefully considered. Children must be (23) _____ in the
(certain)
knowledge that they are loved. Parents should (24) _____
(reserve)
time to spend exclusively with their children, and children should be able to (25) _____ with the demands that their parents make of
(deal)
them.

F. Topics for Discussion and Composition

1. Many latchkey children are mature and can handle their free time productively. Conversely, some youngsters are very apprehensive or fearful about this time alone. What suggestions can you make to help children alleviate these negative feelings?
2. What would you advise parents to do if their children broke the rules that their parents had set—for example, inviting friends to the house when it was forbidden?
3. What emergencies might arise while latchkey children are alone? How can parents prepare their children for these possibilities?
4. What can parents do with their children to make the most of their limited time together?
5. What procedure is it advisable to follow in order to set up fair arrangements for latchkey children? For example, should older children have more privileges than younger children?

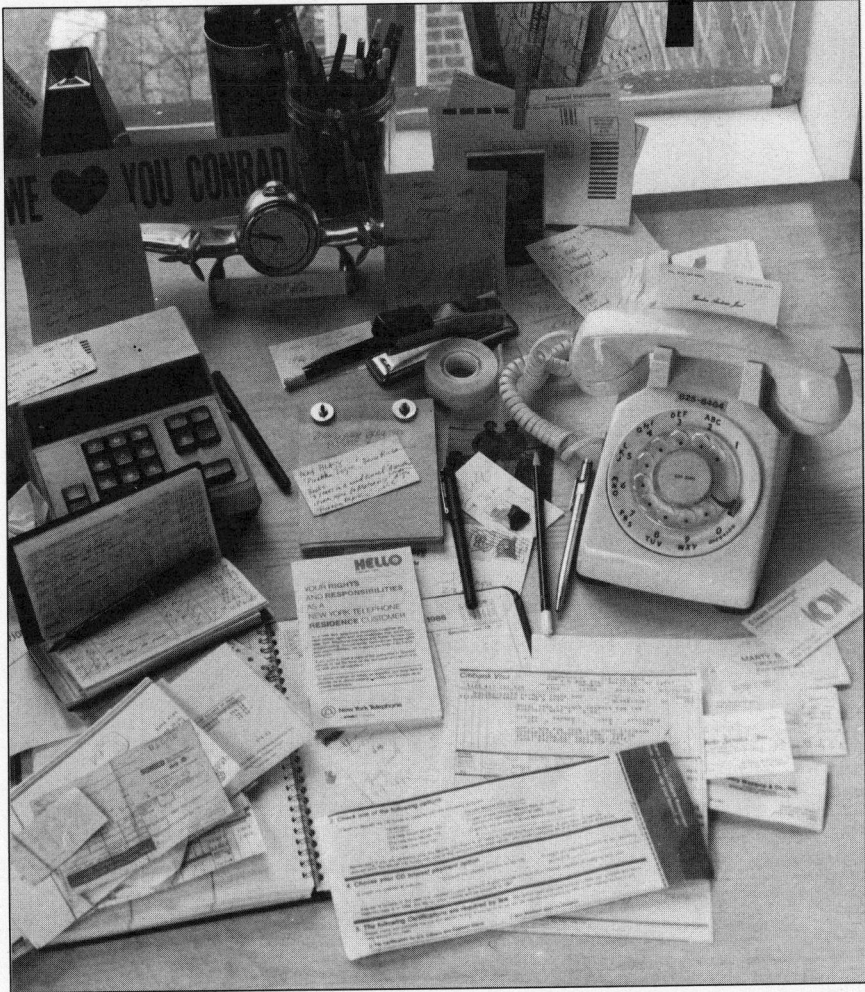

Getting Organized:
Where Did I Put
My Keys?

Introductory Questions

1. Do you admire some people for their orderliness and neatness? What exactly is it that impresses you about them?
2. Do you feel that you are an organized person? In what ways are you organized? In what ways are you disorganized?
3. If you feel that you are disorganized, what changes would you like to make? How would you make these changes?

Getting Organized: Where Did I Put My Keys?

Do you carefully save all kinds of papers, but then you don't remember where you put them? Do you misplace your keys or gloves frequently? Are your closets cluttered, so you can never find what you want? Do you **accumulate** newspapers and magazines, and never find the time to read them? Is your
5 room generally a mess? Do you frequently run out of soap, bread, toothpaste, time, money?

If you fit this description, your life is probably quite **disorganized.** As a result, you tend to **waste** time, add **pressure** to your life, and become frustrated with all the chaos, or disorder, you encounter daily.
10 Don't despair! Your life *can* become more orderly and **efficient.** Disorder does not have to be a permanent condition. The first important step in making improvements is to decide that you want to change. When you are ready to make changes, the second step is to write down exactly what it is that causes you problems. It's important to be specific. For example, a list of
15 your exact problems might include:

1. I'm always running out of such staples as bread, rice, coffee, tea, and so on. How can I plan more effectively to have these basic food items always on hand?
2. I'm always rushing to get ready in the morning, and I'm always late for
20 work. How can I make the mornings less hectic while still getting to work **on time?**
3. The bedroom is always messed up with clothes on chairs and on the floor, and I can never find what I want to wear. What can I do?

By writing down the problem, you define, or identify, it; this is a basic step.
25 Limit yourself to six conditions that you wish to change. More than six is **overwhelming,** and you will become discouraged by the size of your list.

The third step is to number each problem from one to six in the order of its negative **impact.** What annoys or irritates you the most is Number 1.

36

Number 6 bothers you the least, so it's a low **priority** item. Some problems
30 are simple, while others are complex. Divide a difficult problem into small,
manageable segments. If your goal is to clean up your bedroom, for example,
think of doing it one section at a time. Straightening out the closet, organizing
the dresser drawers, vacuuming the rug, and cleaning under the bed are four
separate tasks that can be done at different times.
35   At this point you have already begun to work on the "bad habits" in
your life. You have identified the issues; you have put them in order of importance; you have broken down the complex problems into manageable
chores. You are now ready for the fourth step: making appointments with
yourself to complete a task on your list. For example, at 10:00 A.M. on Sat-
40 urday, you will clean out your bedroom closet. Obviously, the fifth step is
keeping your appointment! Empty the closet completely. Discard everything
you have not worn or used in the past two years. Be firm! Put back what you
have decided to keep. Put similar articles together, i.e., hang all shirts on the
left and suits on the right. Arrange all folded sweaters on one shelf. Having
45 done this, you will see an immediate improvement. Not only have you organized your closet, but you have also **facilitated** finding what you want to wear.
Getting dressed in the morning will take less time.
    Here are some general helpful hints to get you started saving time:

1. Be efficient and do two things at once. For example, exercise or shine your
50   shoes or sew while watching TV. Write a letter or read a book while wait-
    ing in the dentist's office.
2. Plan in advance. To save time in the morning, set out your clothes and
    breakfast dishes the night before. If you do much writing, reading, sewing,
    painting, and so on, set aside an area that is comfortable and pleasant for
55   these activities. Provide drawers, shelves, boxes, and folders to hold var-
    ious articles and supplies you need. Sometimes a decorative object can
    serve a functional purpose. A ceramic mug can hold pens and pencils;
    attractive baskets can be **receptacles** for bills, letters, or notes. Use a spe-
    cial place for specific items, and **eliminate clutter.**
60 3. If you have difficulty remembering appointments and birthdays or anni-
    versaries, a large calendar on the wall will solve that particular problem.
    At the beginning of the year, write all special dates in the **appropriate**
    boxes; write in appointments as you make them. A **glance** at the calendar
    will bring to your attention what is coming up.
65 4. Always perform a task in the location that has been planned for it. For
    instance, get into the habit of opening mail at your desk or in the area set
    aside for writing and paperwork. Do not sit in the living room when you
    open your mail. You will create either clutter if you leave papers there, or
    extra handling by transferring bills to the writing area where your check-
70   book and stamps are.

    As far as papers are concerned, they belong in one of three categories:
    (1) paper such as junk mail, to throw away; (2) paper such as bills, to act on;
    (3) paper such as bank statements, to file away temporarily. Be sure not to

hang onto papers that should be discarded. *You* know the difference between
75 what should be kept and what is useless. Don't save the useless. Plan time to
work on papers that require action. Make an appointment with yourself to
write a letter, reply to an invitation, pay bills. Important papers that must be
kept should be placed in the appropriate file, box, drawer, or folder. Keep a
wastebasket handy for the papers that should go there.
80   Once you are organized, you will have more spare time for yourself.
Your life will be less hectic. You will be pleased with what you have accomplished, and will have more time to spend singing in the shower!

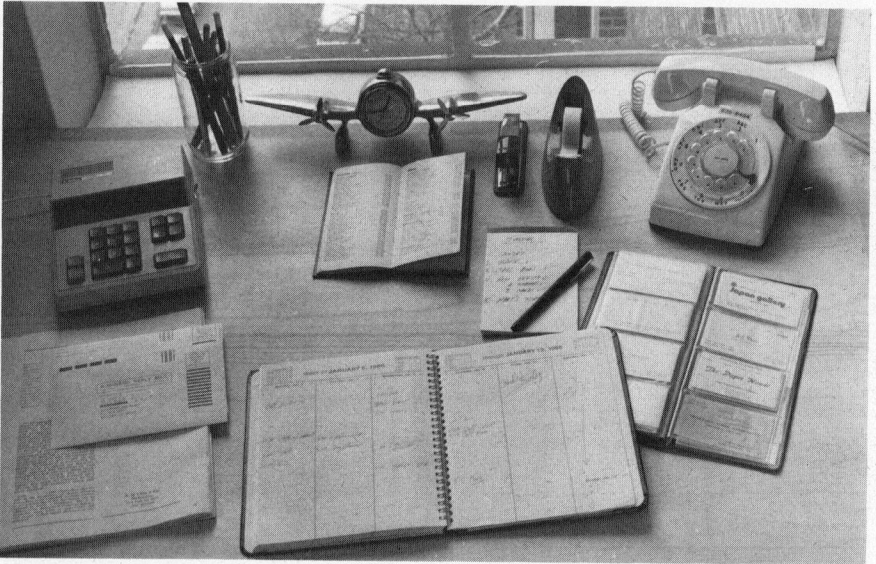

A. True/False Statements

After reading the passage for the first time, read the following statements and
check whether they are True (T) or False (F).

_____ T _____ F   1. It is too difficult for messy people to become orderly;
therefore, they shouldn't even try.

_____ T _____ F   2. If you are not going to make a total change, don't even
bother to start.

_____ T _____ F   3. Identifying the exact problem is a necessary basic step.

_____ T _____ F   4. It is efficient to make a decorative, or pretty, object
serve a useful function.

_____ T _____ F   5. It doesn't matter *where* a task gets done, as long as it gets done.

_____ T _____ F   6. Organized people can easily locate whatever they need.

B. Comprehension Questions

1. The main idea of the article is:
   a. It is possible to become organized once a person is ready to face the problem.
   b. Disorganized people can become efficient by following a step-by-step plan.
   c. Many people are disorganized and need to do something about it.
   d. Becoming organized after living a messy lifestyle requires considerable intelligence.
2. Once you have seriously decided to become organized, what is the first action you take?
3. Why isn't it a good idea to make a long list of problems you want to eliminate?
4. What is the most effective way to handle one big problem you choose to get rid of?
5. There is a saying: "A place for everything, and everything in its place." Why is this idea important?
6. Accumulation of papers is a primary cause of clutter. How can this particular problem be dealt with?

C. Vocabulary in Context Exercise: Part I

A. Read the sentences below carefully, and try to understand the meaning of the boldface words.
   1. Susan's desk is full of old letters, canceled checks, stationery, stamps, paper clips, and bills. Because of all this **clutter,** Susan is never able to find anything quickly or easily.
   2. Mrs. Winter's secretary is very **efficient.** He knows his job well and does it accurately and quickly.
   3. Tom was very heavy, and wanted to lose weight, so he went on a diet. He started by **eliminating** cake, cookies, and candy, all of which he had been eating every day. Instead, he ate fresh fruit.
   4. Mary was too shy to look directly at her date, so she **glanced** at him occasionally while they rode the bus to the restaurant.
   5. When John was twelve years old, he saw a plane crash and catch fire. This experience had such a frightening **impact** on him that he has never been in a plane. He has never even gone to an airport.

6. The doctor quickly examined the woman who had been injured in a car accident. She had a broken leg and a cut on her face; she had also stopped breathing. The doctor's **priority** was getting her to breathe again.

7. The little girl used a glass jar as a **receptacle** for the colorful butterfly that she had caught.

B. Match the following words with the definitions and synonyms listed below.

clutter	eliminate	impact	receptacle
efficient	glance	priority	

1. _____ : something needing attention in preference to something else

2. _____ : container

3. _____ : look quickly; look briefly

4. _____ : strong effect; force of impression; shock

5. _____ : remove; get rid of

6. _____ : effective; competent

7. _____ : condition of collected objects that are not in order

C. Vocabulary in Context Exercise: Part II

A. Read the sentences below carefully, and try to understand the meaning of the boldface words.

1. I never throw away anything. I always put newspapers, old clothes, and broken appliances in the basement. Since I never clean out my basement, so many useless objects have **accumulated** there that I have no more space to put anything.

2. If you are invited to someone's home for dinner, it is **appropriate** to bring a bottle of wine, some fresh flowers, or a small box of cookies. It would not be **appropriate** to bring your own dinner.

3. Lee is very **disorganized** about paying his bills. Sometimes he pays them every month, but often he forgets for two or three months. When he does pay his bills, sometimes he pays cash, while at other times he writes a check. When he pays by check, he frequently forgets to write it in his checkbook, so he sometimes pays the same bill twice.

4. Registering for school the first time is a very complicated process. In order to **facilitate** this long, confusing process, make an appointment to see your advisor. She will explain the procedure clearly and simply to you, and you will save time and energy.

5. The trains in my city are always **on time.** If the train is due at 12:02, it will surely arrive at 12:02, not 12:03. I can depend on it.
6. When Walter began school, he was **overwhelmed** by the amount of work he was required to do. He had to study a chapter a night for all five of his subjects. He had a test in each subject every week, and a report every month, in addition to four oral presentations for the term.
7. Carol was under considerable **pressure** to do well in her new job. She was the first woman hired by the company, so the management was watching her closely to see if she could handle the work. If she could not, she would be fired, and no more women would be hired.
8. Cathy has a terrible habit. She **wastes** money. She buys clothes that she never wears. She also enjoys going out to eat, but she goes to expensive restaurants, and then eats only half the food she orders. She takes taxis everywhere, even when the bus is convenient. She never thinks about saving money, or about spending it more wisely.

B. Match the following words with the definitions and synonyms listed below.

accumulate	disorganized	on time	pressure
appropriate	facilitate	overwhelm	waste

1. _____ : unsystematic; confused

2. _____ : punctual; on schedule

3. _____ : squander; thoughtlessly spend energy, time, money, and so on

4. _____ : collect; gather together

5. _____ : overpower; overcome; upset; disturb

6. _____ : make easier; make less difficult

7. _____ : suitable; proper

8. _____ : stress; tension

D. Detailed Comprehension Exercise

Answer the following questions. Refer back to the passage wherever necessary.

1. "Do you misplace your keys or gloves frequently?" (line 2)

   Look at the parts of the word *misplace*. What does **misplace** mean? _____
2. "Is your room generally a mess?" (lines 4–5)

   a. What does **generally** mean? _____

   b. How do you know? _____

3. "Do you frequently run out of soap, bread, toothpaste, time, money?" (lines 5–6)

   a. What does **run out of** mean? _____

   b. How do you know? _____

4. "If you fit this description, your life is probably quite disorganized. As a result, you tend to waste time, add pressure to your life, and become frustrated with all the chaos, or disorder, you encounter daily." (lines 7–9)

   a. How does *as a result* connect what follows it to what precedes it?

   _____

   b. What does **chaos** mean? _____

   c. How do you know? _____

5. "When you are ready to make changes, the second step is to write down exactly what it is that causes you problems. It's important to be specific." (lines 12–14)

   What word in these sentences is synonymous with **exact**? _____

6. "I'm always running out of such staples as bread, rice, coffee, tea, and so on. How can I plan more effectively to have these basic food items always on hand?" (lines 16–18)

   a. What is the relationship between the words *bread, rice, coffee, tea*

   and the word *staple?* _____

   b. How do you know? _____

   c. What is the meaning of the word **staple?** _____

   d. How do you know? _____

   e. What does **on hand** mean? _____

   f. How do you know? _____

7. "I'm always rushing to get ready in the morning, and I'm always late for work. How can I make the mornings less hectic while still getting to work on time?" (lines 19–21)

   a. What does **hectic** mean? _____

   b. How do you know? _____

8. "By writing down the problem, you define, or identify, it." (line 24)

   a. What does **define** mean? _____

   b. How do you know? _____

9. "Some problems are simple, while others are complex. Divide a difficult problem into small, manageable segments." (lines 29–31)

a. What does **while** mean? _____

b. What does **segments** mean? _____

c. How do you know? _____

10. "At this point you have already begun to work on the 'bad habits' in your life." (lines 35–36)

Why is *bad habits* in quotation marks? _____

11. " . . . you have broken down the complex problems into manageable chores. You are now ready for the fourth step: making appointments with yourself to complete a task on your list." (lines 37–39)

a. Which word in these sentences is synonymous with *tasks*? _____

b. How do you know? _____

12. "Empty the closet completely. Discard everything you have not worn or used in the past two years. . . . Put back what you have decided to keep." (lines 41–43)

a. What does **discard** mean? _____

b. How do you know? _____

13. "Put similar articles together, i.e., hang all shirts on the left and suits on the right." (lines 43–44)

a. What does **i.e.,** mean? _____

b. How do you know? _____

14. "Not only have you organized your closet, but you have also facilitated finding what you want to wear." (lines 45–46)
How do *not only* and *but also* connect the two parts of this sentence?

_____

15. ". . . do two things at once. For example, exercise or shine your shoes or sew while watching TV." (lines 49–50)

a. What does **at once** mean in this context? _____

b. How do you know? _____

16. "Plan in advance. To save time in the morning, set out your clothes and breakfast dishes the night before." (lines 52–53)

a. What does **in advance** mean? _____

b. How do you know? _____

17. "Always perform a task in the location that has been planned for it. For instance, get into the habit of opening mail at your desk or in the area set aside for writing and paperwork." (lines 65–67)

a. What does **for instance** mean? _____

b. How do you know? _____

18. "Be sure not to hang onto papers that should be discarded." (lines 73–74)

    a. What does **hang onto** mean? _____

    b. How do you know? _____

E. Vocabulary in Context Quiz

Complete each blank space with a synonym of the word(s) in parentheses. You may need to use more than one word.

    Do you always know where your keys are? Are your closets

(1)_____, or are you the rare person who always keeps every-
        (crowded)
thing in good order?

    Very many of us are (2) _____ in one area or another,
                  (unsystematic)
and we (3) _____ dislike this characteristic in ourselves.
        (usually)
Being disorganized in many ways leads to (4) _____, which
                 (disorder)
prevents a person from having a calm, satisfying life.

    A person whose life is quite disorganized (5) _____
                    (squanders)
much time, creates unnecessary (6) _____, and feels over-
              (stress)
come by clutter.

    It is possible, however, to correct this undesirable

(7) _____ of living. The first move is to make a firm decision
      (way)
to change some of your bad habits. Write down on paper the

(8) _____ behavior patterns that recur often, and be
     (annoying)
(9) _____. For example:
     (exact)
1. I'm always (10) _____ toothpaste. How can I plan more
          (running short of)
(11) _____?
   (efficiently)

2. I never leave the house (12) _____ in the morning. How
(punctually)
can I avoid getting to work late?

It's important to (13) _____ your problems in this way,
(identify)
but begin with a maximum of six problems. A longer list could prove

(14) _____, and you might give up trying to improve.
(overpowering)
Among   the   problems   you   list,   some   will   be   more

(15) _____ than others. Divide these problems into smaller
(difficult)
(16) _____. For instance, if a messy desk is your problem,
(parts)
clean out one drawer at a time instead of trying to do the entire desk at once.

Examine   your   list   of   problems   to   see   which   ones   are   very

(17) _____ and which are less bothersome. Number the most
(irritating)
serious problem Number 1 and the least serious problem Number 6. Give

your attention to Number 1 first. The less important problems can wait.

Now   make   a(n) (18)_____ with yourself to complete
(date)
your   first   assignment.   Perhaps   you   can   do   two   things

(19) _____. For   example,   you   can   iron   your   clothes
(at the same time)
while watching TV. Planning (20) _____ is also helpful.
(ahead of time)
Put out your clothing for the next day before you go to bed. This procedure

saves time in the morning. A large calendar can help you remember

dates like appointments, birthdays, and so on. Make notes in the

(20) _____   spaces,   and   (22) _____   at
(proper)   (quickly look)
the calendar to see what is coming up.

Try to do a (23) _____ at the place that you have set
(chore)
aside for that purpose. It will help keep your home or workplace neat.

Paper is something most of us collect and save, and much of it is useless.

Have the strength to (24) _____ papers you know you have
(throw away)
no need for.

Being organized saves time, and makes you (25) _____
(competent)
and happy!

F. Topics for Discussion and Composition

1. What annoying habit do you have that you would like to eliminate? Why do you want to eliminate this particular habit?
2. Old habits are difficult to change. Can you think of why you developed this habit in the first place?
3. What has made you continue in this manner even though you dislike it?
4. The article made several suggestions on how to clear up organization problems. Discuss some other steps you can take to become more organized.

What's New?
The Media

Introductory Questions

1. How do we find out what is happening in our city and in other cities?
2. How does news from distant parts of the world get to us?
3. If we have little time and want just the highlights, or major events, in the news, what source is the best?
4. If we want details of current events, and perhaps some diverse opinions about the news, what source is the best?
5. How can we learn if a news report is accurate?

What's New? The Media

Revolutionary inventions in the field of communications enable news from all over the world to be reported everywhere instantaneously. This spectacular development affects our lives considerably. It is as though the whole world were in our own backyard. What is new across the ocean comes to our atten-
5 tion just as speedily as what is new in our neighborhood. We can readily see, hear, and read about what goes on worldwide.

People who gather, describe, and **interpret** news are called reporters, or journalists. Reporters work for every medium, or method, of communication: newspapers, magazines, radio, television. The media have become very
10 **influential** in our lives. Each medium has its advantages and disadvantages; each is important in our society.

Television is the favorite medium of communication of many people. Seeing a royal wedding or watching a spacecraft take off brings the viewer right into the action. Seeing and hearing a politician speak gives the feeling
15 of knowing the person. It requires little effort to watch television, and it is usually done in the comfort of one's home.

Newspapers report news in greater detail than television does. There are fewer pictures, however, and there is a longer time lapse, or lag, between the occurrence of an event and the delivery of papers to the newsstands. Most
20 papers carry local, state, national, and international news.

Radio is a simple, convenient means of keeping abreast of what is going on in the world. News is relayed by eyewitness reporters at the scene of the event. They are there as the action occurs. Furthermore, the radio can be listened to while riding in a car, working in a factory or office, walking in the
25 street, or sitting at home. There is no visual **aspect** to radio reporting.

News magazines review the news of the week in great detail, include pictures, and often present commentaries, consequences, and **controversies.**

In the United States, information from all over the world is collected by the media via two giant "wire services," United Press International (UPI) and

30 Associated Press (AP). These wire services have reporters working throughout
the nation and the world. They constantly feed news across the wires to various news centers. The wire services are a major source of news for the media. These **sources** are **supplemented** by each medium's own reporters. In
addition, government agencies, universities, and large corporations issue
35 news items. These written reports are called press releases.

Since the media are independent, **profit**-making organizations, they are
not funded by the government. Of course, when we buy newspapers and
magazines, we help **defray** the costs of running this **vast** business, but this is
a very small source of income for these companies. The advertisements in
40 newspapers and magazines and the commercials on radio and television provide a **substantial** source of income.

Each medium has editors who are responsible for the final form of the
news reports. Editors review the material that reporters submit, determine
how the news will be reported, how much of it to report, and which item will
45 be the headline story. Editors are responsible for what news and how much
news is presented in their papers or programs. They set the standards for the
quality and tone of the paper or broadcast. For example, some editors focus
on sensationalism, while others present current events in a serious, objective
way. Finally, editors must also take care to eliminate any grammatical or
50 spelling errors a reporter may make before the stories "go to press."

The ideal reporter is **inquisitive,** aggressive, diplomatic, and swift. They
are in competition with each other to get the scoop, i.e., to be first with the
news. Some reporters become specialists in a certain area, such as finance,
medicine, international news, or sports. Television reporters may become ce-
55 lebrities, since the public actually sees them on the screen. A name printed
in a newspaper byline does not have the same impact as a person seen and
heard on a television screen.

Accuracy is a primary goal in journalism. Since the media also emphasize speed in reporting, there often is no time to **verify** the information that
60 comes through. Facts are gathered quickly, organized, put into print, pictures, or speech for the public with great rapidity. Sometimes there are errors, but they are the result of haste, not deliberate falsification. Another
problem that frequently arises is the excessive attention that many people in
the public eye receive. Many of them complain that the media invade their
65 privacy by constantly having reporters and photographers following them to
report their activities.

Objectivity is an equally important aim. People in management are, of
course, entitled to express their own opinions. These opinions are, however,
reserved for editorial columns. The media have been very competent in in-
70 vestigative reporting. They help **detect** and **expose** corruption, incompetence,
and bribe taking in government as well as in private industry. They have been
especially effective because of their objectivity.

An interesting way to learn more about journalism is to compare the
same news story as reported by the different media and then analyze how
75 rival broadcasting stations or competing newspapers **deal with** it. The differ-

ences will give you **insight** into how the judgment of the editors shape the
final presentation of a news report.

    Life today is fast-moving and complex. A well-informed, well-educated
society can surely make sounder, more practical decisions than an ignorant
80 one. Responsible media and competent journalists make vital contributions to
such a society.

A. True/False Statements

After reading the passage for the first time, read the following statements and
check whether they are True (T) or False (F).

_____ T _____ F   1. In the twentieth century, local news and international
news are reported with equal speed.

_____ T _____ F   2. The quickest way to learn the latest news is to pick up
a newspaper at the newsstand.

_____ T _____ F   3. The media are not independent agencies; they depend
on the government for funding, or money.

_____ T _____ F   4. Because television reporters are in the public eye, they
often become famous and popular.

_____ T _____ F   5. The media rarely, if ever, publicize the private lives of
individuals.

_____ T _____ F   6. All news media present events in exactly the same way.

B. Comprehension Questions

1. The main idea of the article is:
   a. News from all around the world travels very rapidly.
   b. People get news from around the world instantly via the mass media.
   c. Radios provide instant access to the news wherever we are.
   d. Of all the media, television is the most entertaining.
2. Why do most people prefer to get their news from television?
3. What traits, or characteristics, must a good reporter have?
4. What traits and skills must a good editor have?
5. What services do UPI and AP provide?
6. How do the various media cover their costs of operation?

C. Vocabulary in Context Exercise: Part I

A. Read the sentences below carefully, and try to understand the meaning of the boldface words.
   1. A well-balanced, nutritious diet is only one **aspect** of being healthy. Exercise, adequate sleep, and avoidance of stress are also important.
   2. Many students must work to pay for their expenses. The money they receive from home is not enough to **defray** the costs of both tuition and living expenses.
   3. The doctor took a blood sample from her patient and sent it to a laboratory for analysis. A rare disease was **detected** in the patient's blood.
   4. The Congressman was forced to resign his position when his bribe-taking practices were **exposed** to the public.
   5. John bought bicycles directly from the company for $100 each. He sold them for $150. His **profit** on each bicycle was $50.
   6. You need a **substantial** amount of money to make a down payment if you buy a house. For example, if you buy a $50,000 house, you will need to pay about $12,000 immediately.
   7. Martha didn't make enough money on her job, so she took a part-time job on weekends in order to **supplement** her income.
   8. The United States is a **vast** country. For example, it would take you several days to cross the United States by car.
B. Match the following words with the definitions and synonyms listed below.

| aspect | detect | profit | supplement |
| defray | expose | substantial | vast |

   1. _____ : gain; benefit

   2. _____ : important; plentiful

   3. _____ : phase; component

   4. _____ : something that makes an addition

5. _____ : disclose; reveal

6. _____ : enormous; tremendous

7. _____ : discover

8. _____ : pay or support the cost of something

C. Vocabulary in Context Exercise: Part II

A. Read the sentences below carefully, and try to understand the meaning of the boldface words.
   1. When you write a composition, be sure to check it for **accuracy.** You may have made a mistake that you didn't notice as you were writing.
   2. Adding pollution-control devices to cars has been a **controversial** issue for years. Environmentalists are in favor of them because they keep air cleaner, but manufacturers don't want to install them because they are expensive.
   3. Some foreign students cannot **deal with** the crowds and the fast pace of life in big cities. They become anxious and unhappy and begin to wish they were home.
   4. An **influential** friend can persuade, or convince, you to do something you might never have thought of doing before.
   5. Cats are very **inquisitive** animals. They love to investigate boxes and bags, for example, and examine anything that moves.
   6. Before you become angry and criticize someone's behavior, stop and think about why he or she acted that way. If you can gain some **insight** into the reasons behind the individual's actions, you may not feel so angry.
   7. There are many ways to **interpret** unusual quietness in an individual. Perhaps the person is worried, shy, uncertain, frightened, preoccupied, or simply tired.
   8. Mary reads through cookbooks as a **source** of new menus and recipes to prepare for her family.
   9. Before you leave on a trip, it is important to **verify** your plane and hotel reservations to be sure they are still valid or in the event any changes have to be made.
B. Match the following words with the definitions and synonyms listed below.

accuracy	deal with	inquisitive	interpret
controversy (n.)	influential	insight	source
controversial (adj.)			verify

1. _____ : confirm; check the accuracy of something

2. _____ : curious

3. _____ : clear understanding of the inner nature of
                        something

4. _____ : handle; manage

5. _____ : explain; bring out the meaning

6. _____ : exactness; correctness

7. _____ : dispute; debate

8. _____ : powerful

9. _____ : origin

D. Detailed Comprehension Exercise

Answer the following questions. Refer back to the passage wherever necessary.

1. "It is as though the whole world were in our own backyard." (line 4)

   a. What is the meaning of this sentence? _____

   b. What does **in our own backyard** mean specifically? _____

   _____

2. "We can readily see, hear, and read about what goes on worldwide." (lines 5–6)

   a. How can we see, hear, and read about *worldwide* news? _____

   _____

   b. From this sentence, what does **readily** mean? _____

3. "People who gather, describe, and interpret news are called reporters, or journalists." (lines 7–8)

   a. What is a synonym for **reporter**? _____

   b. How do you know this word is a synonym? _____

4. "Reporters work for every medium, or method, of communication. . . ." (lines 8–9)

   a. What is a synonym of **medium**? _____

   b. How do you know this word is a synonym? _____

5. "The media have become very influential in our lives." (lines 9–10)
   a. What is the connection between the words *media* and *medium?*

   _____

   b. How do you know? _____

   _____

6. " . . . there is a longer time lapse, or lag, between the occurrence of an event and the delivery of papers to the newsstands." (lines 18–19)

   What does **time lapse** or **time lag** mean? _____

   _____

7. "Radio is a simple, convenient means of keeping abreast of what is going on in the world." (lines 21–22)

   What does **keep abreast of** mean? _____

8. "Furthermore, the radio can be listened to while riding in a car, . . ." (lines 23–24)
   Read all of paragraph 5. How does *furthermore* relate what precedes it

   to what follows it? _____

   _____

9. Read paragraph 7. In line 29, what does **via** mean?

   _____

10. "In addition, government agencies, universities, and large corporations issue news items. These are called press releases." (lines 33–35)

What are **press releases?** _____

11. "Since the media are independent, profit-making organizations, they are not funded by the government." (lines 36 – 37)

   a. What does **since** mean in this sentence? _____

   b. How is the first part of this sentence related to the second part?

   _____

12. "The advertisements in newspapers and magazines and the commercials on radio and television provide a substantial source of income." (lines 39 – 41)

   a. How are **advertisements** and **commercials** similar? _____

   b. How are they different? _____

   _____

13. "Editors . . . determine . . . which item will be the headline story." (lines 43 – 45)
   What is a **headline story?**

   _____

14. "Editors must . . . eliminate any . . . errors . . . before the stories 'go to press.' " (lines 49 – 50)

   What does **go to press** mean?_____
15. "They are in competition with each other to get the scoop, i.e., to be first with the news." (lines 51 – 53)

   a. What does it mean **to get the scoop?** _____

   _____

   b. How do you know? In other words, what does **i.e.,** mean?

   _____

16. "A name printed in a newspaper byline does not have the same impact as a person seen and heard on a television screen." (lines 55 – 57)

   What is a **newspaper byline?** _____
17. "Sometimes there are errors, but they are the result of haste, not deliberate falsification." (lines 61 – 62)

   What does **falsification** mean? _____
18. Read lines 63 – 64. Who are **people in the public eye?**

   _____

19. "The media have been very competent in investigative reporting. They help detect and expose corruption, incompetence, and bribe taking in government as well as in private industry." (lines 69 – 71)

What is **investigative reporting?** _____

_____

_____

E. Vocabulary in Context Quiz

Complete each blank space with a synonym of the word(s) in parentheses. You may need to use more than one word.

The remarkable devices of communication in the twentieth century make it possible for news to be reported (1)_____ all over the
(without delay)
world. We can get news via several (2) _____ such as radio,
(methods of communication)
television, and newspapers. Each presents news in different ways, and each has its (3) _____ as well as weak points.
(benefits)
Television is the most popular medium for news reports. Seeing and hearing what goes on makes viewers feel as though they are eye witnesses to the events.

Newspaper reports are more (4) _____ than television
(thorough)
reports. However, there is a long time (5) _____ between the
(lag)
event and the printing of it in the papers.

Radio enables us to keep (6)_____ news very easily.
(informed of)
Portable radios and car radios provide access to the news wherever we are, but radio lacks the visual (7) _____ that television offers.
(component)
News magazines present a detailed review of the week's events. Usually, they publish all points of view when reporting (8) _____ issues. After reading this material, we gain more
(debatable)
(9) _____ into the issues.
(understanding)
In the United States, two huge wire services are in the business of (10) _____ news. The media use these wire services as
(gathering)

(11) _____ of news. They also (12) _____
　　　　(origins)　　　　　　　　　　　　　　　　　　　(add to)
these origins by having reporters of their own working for them.

　　The media are not supported financially by the government. They are

in business independently and for (13) _____. When people
　　　　　　　　　　　　　　　　　　　　　　(gain)
buy newspapers or magazines, they help (14) _____ the costs
　　　　　　　　　　　　　　　　　　　　　　　(support)
of running the business. A (15) _____ portion of their income
　　　　　　　　　　　　　　　　(plentiful)
is derived from advertising. (16) _____ sums of money are
　　　　　　　　　　　　　　　　(Enormous)
involved in the advertising business.

　　A competent reporter is alert, (17) _____, aggres-
　　　　　　　　　　　　　　　　　　　　(curious)
sive, and swift. Reporters working on television become

(18) _____ because they are repeatedly seen by the public.
　　(famous, popular people)
News is transmitted with such (19) _____ that some-
　　　　　　　　　　　　　　　　　(speed)
times errors are made. It is the editor's job to (20) _____ and
　　　　　　　　　　　　　　　　　　　　　　　　(discover)
correct them. Reporters aim for (21) _____ and are care-
　　　　　　　　　　　　　　　　　(exactness)
ful to avoid the falsification of reports. Rather, they try

to (22) _____ their information before the paper
　　　　(confirm)
(23) _____ . Although objectivity is a priority with
　　　(is printed)
(24) _____ , the opinions of editors are
　　　(journalists)
(25) _____ in the shaping of the final report.
　　　(powerful)
Life today is complex. A responsible system of communication enables

the public to participate in the making of history.

F. Topics for Discussion and Composition

1. In some countries, the government controls the media. In the United States and other countries, the media are private corporations. What are the advantages and disadvantages of each system?
2. In the United States, reporters are not required to report their source of information in order to protect those sources. Are there any circumstances where you think such sources should be revealed?
3. In the United States, the media are dependent on the business community for financial support. How could this affect (a) what is printed; and (b) the truth of what is printed?
4. What is a broadcast? What is the difference between a paper and a broadcast? What are the advantages and disadvantages of each?
5. In terms of news reporting, what is sensationalism? How does sensationalism affect the way people perceive the news?

Burning Up Money
and Yourself

Introductory Questions

1. What is a habit? What are some examples of good habits? bad habits?
2. Do you have habits you would like to break? What are they? Why would you like to break these habits?
3. What is the biggest difficulty for you in breaking a habit?
4. Do you know of habits that are especially hard to break because you feel physically uncomfortable when you try to stop? What do you call these habits?

Burning Up Money and Yourself

"Tomorrow" is always the most convenient time to start breaking an old, comfortable, established habit. Most of us have started working on a basic change in our behavior on many "tomorrows" without much success. Good intentions are there, but **willpower** is not.

5   Some habits that we cultivate are actually detrimental to our health, and doctors advise that we "break" these habits. Smoking is one of the most highly **publicized** bad habits. Doctors frequently tell their patients, "Quit smoking." This advice is sensible from several standpoints, such as health, money, and cleanliness, and it prompts a serious resolution to give up this unhealthful
10   habit.

In an hour or two, however, the smoker feels **grouchy**, his hands start to tremble, or shake, and cigarettes are on his mind. It is not going to be easy to break this habit. In fact, it is very difficult because smoking has become an addiction—the body has become **addicted** to the nicotine in cigarettes. Each
15   inhalation sends a **dose** of nicotine to the brain via the bloodstream. This nicotine brings on the release of **hormones** that cause the heartbeat to **accelerate** and blood pressure to rise. The smoker feels relaxed and can **concentrate** well. In a short time, however, the nicotine level in the blood **diminishes,** giving rise to **withdrawal** symptoms: nervousness, **jitters,** and a **craving**
20   for another cigarette. It becomes a vicious cycle: smoking causes craving, which causes smoking, and so on.

Many experiments have demonstrated the fact that nicotine is addictive. Cigarette companies, however, do not include this feature in their **abundant** ads. In experiments, regular smokers who were **surreptitiously** switched to
25   low-nicotine cigarettes resorted to various techniques to increase the amount of nicotine they inhaled: they smoked more cigarettes than usual, left smaller

60

butts in ashtrays, inhaled more deeply, and held the smoke in their lungs for a longer time.

Whether a smoker quits gradually or goes "cold turkey," there will be
30 suffering. Typical withdrawal symptoms are irritability, tension, difficulty in concentrating, **fatigue,** tendency to overeat, inability to sleep, and intense craving for another cigarette. Since the gradual as well as the abrupt method of quitting smoking causes suffering, it is probably advisable to endure this pain for a shorter duration and go cold turkey.
35 The following are helpful suggestions for this difficult period:

1. Promise yourself you won't smoke at all for just one week. This limited time is a more reasonable goal than "forever." It will be a rough week, but it will pass. **Persevere!**
2. Inform all people you associate with, like family, co-workers, and so on,
40 that you are engaged in this project and that you may be a little irritated.
3. If you weaken and must have a cigarette, don't stop at one. Have many— enough to make you sick.
4. Keep very busy during this period of **transition.** Do exercises, take long walks, visit friends, make or fix things with your hands. Chewing gum and
45 drinking plenty of water are helpful, too.

Within two to four weeks almost all withdrawal symptoms will disappear, along with the craving for cigarettes. For some people it is helpful to join a group having the same goal. It takes much **discipline** to quit smoking, but with enough willpower, every smoker can succeed in becoming a non-
50 smoker.

A. True/False Statements

After reading the passage for the first time, read the following statements and check whether they are True (T) or False (F).

_____ T _____ F   1. Many people would like to break bad habits, but they do not have enough self-control.

_____ T _____ F   2. Sometimes we develop habits that are actually harmful to our health.

_____ T _____ F   3. Most people can give up smoking without any difficulty.

_____ T _____ F   4. Quitting smoking all at once will cause more suffering than quitting slowly and gradually.

_____ T _____ F   5. The period during which a person is giving up cigarettes is a very difficult time for her, as well as her friends and associates.

_____ T _____ F   6. The person who quits smoking will certainly start smoking again in a short time.

B. Comprehension Questions

1. The main idea of the article is:
   a. Many people want to break habits, but it is very difficult.
   b. Although many people find it difficult to break habits, it *is* possible.
   c. Many people have a variety of habits, both good and bad.
   d. Many people smoke, which is a very bad habit to have.
2. What is the difference between a habit and an addiction?
3. Some people are habitual smokers. What good feelings do they get from smoking cigarettes?
4. What happens to a habitual smoker when he or she hasn't had a cigarette for over an hour?
5. What are some methods one can use to end an addiction?

C. Vocabulary in Context Exercise: Part I

A. Read the sentences below carefully, and try to understand the meaning of the boldface words.
   1. The little boy had a **craving** for chocolate. He spent all his money to buy chocolate candy, and he would eat only chocolate ice cream.

2. Harry worked in the Complaint Department. After listening to angry people all day, he felt very **grouchy** when he came home and shouted at his wife because dinner wasn't ready.

3. Many people experience the **jitters** when they have an important job interview or an important test to take. They feel very **jittery** and become relaxed only when the day is over.

4. Fast-food restaurants are **abundant** in the United States. There seems to be one on every street in every city and several next to every highway!

5. Dennis asked Carol to marry him, and she said yes. Their engagement was **publicized** in the society column of the local newspaper.

6. The government agent **surreptitiously** took photographs of the enemy's planes and airfield. If she had been caught, she would have been killed as a spy.

7. The young couple found it very difficult to make the **transition** from living a quiet life in the country to living a busy life in the city.

8. Ann was on a diet. She wanted to lose ten pounds. It took her a great deal of **willpower** not to eat cake for dessert when her whole family was sitting at the same table with her, enjoying their chocolate cake.

9. The heroin addict experienced extreme discomfort during his **withdrawal** from the drug. He kept up his courage, however, because he did not want to be an addict any more.

B. Match the following words with the definitions and synonyms listed below.

abundant	grouchy	publicize	transition	withdrawal
craving	jitters (n.)	surreptitiously	willpower	
	jittery (adj.)			

1. _____ : advertise; make known

2. _____ : extreme nervousness

3. _____ : the process of giving up the use of a drug or other substance on which one has become dependent

4. _____ : intense desire; yearning

5. _____ : bad-tempered; irritable

6. _____ : secretly

7. _____ : numerous; plentiful; prolific

8. _____ : change

9. _____ : self-control

C. Vocabulary in Context Exercise: Part II

A. Read the sentences below carefully, and try to understand the meaning of the boldface words.
1. As the train left the station, it **accelerated** to sixty miles an hour.
2. The woman was **addicted** to sleeping pills. She could not go to sleep without taking two every night.
3. Stanley tried to **concentrate** on doing his homework but the noise from his brother's radio kept distracting him. He would look at his book but listen to the music and news from the radio.
4. John had $50.00 to spend on groceries. As he went from store to store, buying meat, vegetables, and other items, the amount of money he had **diminished.** By the time he arrived home, he had only $1.75 left.
5. It takes a great deal of **discipline** to become an athlete. You must work out every day even if you are tired. In addition, you must eat a careful diet and avoid certain foods. Furthermore, you cannot stay out late at night, smoke, or drink.
6. The doctor told her patient to take one spoonful of medicine three times a day. She told him not to change this **dose** without calling her first to discuss it.
7. Although the runner was in excellent condition, by the end of the twenty-five-mile race, he experienced a strong sense of **fatigue.** He rested and slept for two days, and his energy returned.
8. Our bodies produce many **hormones,** which are necessary for our good health. They circulate in our bodies and affect the activity of the cells.
9. The teenager wanted to get a driver's license very badly, but he failed the driving test. He took the test three more times but failed repeatedly. He **persevered,** however, and the fifth time he passed.

B. Match the following words with the definitions and synonyms listed below.

accelerate   concentrate   discipline   fatigue   persevere
addicted   diminish   dose   hormone

1. _____ : a substance produced in an organ of the body

2. _____ : physically dependent on something, for example, drugs

3. _____ : tiredness; exhaustion

4. _____ : become faster; speed up

5. _____ : persist; continue steadily in a course of action

6. _____ : amount or quantity of something, such as a medicine or drug

7. _____ : lessen; decrease

8. _____ : focus attention

9. _____ : control

D. Detailed Comprehension Exercise

Answer the following questions. Refer back to the passage wherever necessary.

1. " 'Tomorrow' is always the most convenient time to start breaking an old, comfortable, established habit." (lines 1–2)
   Why is the word *tomorrow* in quotation marks?

   _____

2. ". . . doctors advise that we 'break' these habits." (line 6)
   Why is the word *break* in quotation marks?

   _____

3. ". . . doctors advise that we 'break' these habits . . . This advice is sensible from several standpoints. . . ." (lines 6–8)
   What is the relationship between *advise* and *advice*?

   _____

4. "This advice is sensible from several standpoints, such as health, money, and cleanliness. . . ." (lines 8–9)

   a. What does **standpoint** mean? _____

   b. How do you know? _____
5. "In an hour or two, however, . . . his hands start to tremble, or shake, and cigarettes are on his mind." (lines 11–12)

   a. What does **tremble** mean? _____

   b. How do you know? _____

   c. What is the meaning of **on one's mind?** _____
6. "It is not going to be easy to break this habit. In fact, it is very difficult because smoking has become an addiction. . . ." (lines 12–14)
   How does *in fact,* relate what precedes it to what follows it?

   _____

7. ". . . the body has become addicted to the nicotine in cigarettes. Each inhalation sends a dose of nicotine to the brain via the bloodstream." (lines 14–15)

   a. According to the sense of the sentence, what does **inhalation** mean?

   _____

b. What does **via** mean? _____

8. "This . . . brings on the release of hormones . . ." (lines 15–16)

What does **brings on** mean? _____

9. "It becomes a vicious cycle: smoking causes craving, which causes smoking, and so on." (lines 20–21)

What is a **vicious cycle?** _____

10. ". . . left smaller butts in ashtrays." (lines 26–27)

What does *butt* refer to? _____

11. "Each inhalation sends a dose of nicotine . . . " (line 15); "the amount of nicotine they inhaled." (lines 25–26)
What is the relationship between **inhalation** and **inhaled?**

_____

12. "Whether a smoker quits gradually or goes 'cold turkey,' there will be suffering." (lines 29–30)

a. What does **cold turkey** mean? _____

b. How do you know? _____

13. "Since the gradual as well as the abrupt method of quitting smoking causes suffering, it is probably advisable to endure this pain for a shorter duration and go cold turkey." (lines 32–34)
a. In this sentence, which word is a synonym for *cold turkey?*

_____

b. How do you know? _____
c. How does the word *advisable* relate to the word *advise* in line 6?

_____

d. What does **since** mean? _____

e. How do you know? _____

f. What does **as well as** mean? _____

14. "Promise yourself you won't smoke at all for just one week. This limited time is a more reasonable goal than 'forever.' " (lines 36–37)

a. Why is *forever* in quotation marks? _____

b. What does the author imply by using quotation marks? _____

_____

15. "Have many—enough to make you sick." (lines 41–42)

How does the dash relate what precedes it to what follows it? _____

_____

16. "Within two to four weeks almost all withdrawal symptoms will disappear, along with the craving for cigarettes." (lines 46–47)

What does **along with** mean? _____

E. Vocabulary in Context Quiz

Complete each blank space with a synonym of the word(s) in parentheses. You may need to use more than one word.

To   break   a   bad   habit   we   need   good   intentions   and

(1) _____, but most people have a short supply of the latter.
    (control)

Some of our habits are actually (2) _____ to our health; smok-
                                     (harmful)

ing is one of them. This fact has been widely (3) _____
                                                    (advertised)

in the media.

When   smokers   decide   to   break   the   habit,   they

(4) _____   a   cigarette   and   are   in   a(n)
    (yearn for)

(5) _____   mood.   They   also   suffer   from
    (irritable)

(6) _____ . It is difficult to summon enough willpower
    (extreme nervousness)

because the body is (7) _____ to nicotine. When smokers
                        (dependent on)

(8) _____ the nicotine in cigarette smoke, the heartbeat
    (breathe in)

(9) _____ and blood pressure rises. They feel relaxed and can
    (speeds up)

(10) _____ . When nicotine is not present in the blood, ner-
     (focus)

vousness and a strong desire for a cigarette set in.

Experiments   have   been   done   in   which   smokers   have

(11) _____ been given low nicotine cigarettes instead of reg-
     (secretly)

ular ones. These people increased the number of cigarettes they smoked,

inhaled more deeply, and left small (12) _____ in their ash-
                                          (unburned cigarette parts)

trays. They needed their (13) _____ of nicotine!
                              (quantity)

Whether   a   smoker   (14) _____   gradually   or
                             (stops)

(15) _____, it is almost always difficult. The following hints
　　　　(abruptly)
may be helpful:

1. Set a goal not to smoke for just one week, and (16) _____;
　　　　　　　　　　　　　　　　　　　　　　　　　　　　　　　(don't give up)
2. Inform everyone of what you are trying to do;

3. If you do have a cigarette, have many—enough to make you

   (17) _____;
   　　(ill)
4. Try to keep busy during this (18) _____. Exercise, visit
   　　　　　　　　　　　　　　　　　　　　(change)
   friends, and so on. Within two to four weeks, the craving for cigarettes

   will (19) _____.
   　　　　(decrease)

   A good dose of (2) _____ can terminate this unhealthy
   　　　　　　　　　　　(self-control)
habit.

F. Topics for Discussion and Composition

1. How does an addiction develop?
2. To eliminate an addiction, which method seems more practical to you:
   gradual withdrawal or cold turkey? Why?
3. Many people choose to work on breaking a habit as a member of a group.
   What are the advantages of this way of breaking a habit?

Day-Care Centers

Introductory Questions

1. What are the advantages and disadvantages of a mother being the sole caretaker of her children?
2. What kind of stimulation can day care provide for children that could not be provided by the average family?
3. What are the most important factors pertinent to the development of a child in the early years?
4. In what ways can a parent promote interaction and socialization for an only child who does not go to day-care centers?

Day-Care Centers

The stereotypical American family of not long ago was comprised of a father who was the breadwinner, a mother who was the homemaker or housewife, and children who were raised for the most part by their mother. During the past two or three decades, however, the term *family* has **evolved** into several
5   **alternate** relationships. While the traditional nuclear family still endures, other family lifestyles have been **proliferating** in modern American society. Surveys show that in homes where both parents of children under six live together, over six million of the mothers work. In other words, for various reasons, both parents work. The number of working mothers rises dramati-
10 cally in families with children under ten years of age. These children gave rise to the creation of the term *latchkey children*. Also significant is the number of single-parent families, which have doubled in the last ten years. The majority of single-parent homes are a consequence of divorce. Death of a spouse accounts for another segment of this category. Parents who are single
15 by choice—a new phenomenon appearing on the American scene—are also included in these statistics.

Along with the evolution of family structures comes the compelling need for organized, accessible, high-quality child care. Just as some present-day necessities such as television, air conditioning, and cars originated as luxuries,
20 day care has shifted from being an option of the well-to-do to a necessity among families in all economic **strata.** In homes where mothers of young children work, it is not uncommon to find a **harried** mother hiring a neighbor two mornings a week and another babysitter five afternoons a week. This arrangement is frequently disrupted by personal emergencies on the part of
25 any one of these people and is **sustained** with great difficulty and much frustration. In fact, a significant number of children are cared for by such unlicensed caretakers as neighbors, relatives and **enterprising** people. Clearly, these families need the reliable services of day-care centers.

Even so, many parents have mixed feelings about leaving their children
30 with strangers as opposed to relatives or friends. They worry about the adverse effects this experience may have on their children. Psychologists, too,
have expressed conflicting views on the value of day-care experiences for
young children. Those who advocate child day care claim that children en-
rolled in these programs learn to perform many tasks by themselves and be-
35 come independent earlier. In addition, their language development is more
advanced, their social skills are more refined, and these children adapt more
easily to playing in groups. They show facility to forming friendships and
learning to be cooperative. When it is time to start elementary school, they
adjust more readily.
40   On the other hand, dissenting psychologists claim that children in poor
or **mediocre** day-care situations are definitely disadvantaged. In centers
where the ratio of children to teachers is very high, children invariably get
inadequate attention. Furthermore, low salaries cause frequent **turnover** in
staff members of some day-care centers. This inconsistency in caretakers up-
45 sets very young children. All doctors, psychologists and laymen agree that a
reliable, constant source of care and attention is vital nourishment for children; the ever-changing staff of many day-care centers does not fill this need.
Physicians note that children in day-care centers come down with **contagious**
ailments frequently. Dissenters claim that high sanitary standards and good
50 hygiene can keep these problems to a minimum. Indeed, exposure to other
children helps youngsters build up **immunity** to disease before they attend
elementary school.
     These objections to day-care centers are valid in some instances; and in
fact, not all centers are acceptable places in which to entrust children. Day-
55 care centers range from being excellent to **mediocre** to **deplorable.** In a mediocre situation, very often the environment is not stimulating or enriching,
and the attention is not personal. **Abominable** conditions prevail in which
despicable sexual abuse of children exists, and children can be seriously disturbed by such experiences. Such situations have recently been exposed in
60 the news, but fortunately they are rare. It is up to the parents to investigate
centers, interview the management, and observe the personnel. It is not
enough to inquire only about the cost of day care. Parents in this situation
are responsible for making a choice that is crucial to their children's development and well-being. The **astute** parent investigates what the center will
65 do for the child. When assessing a child-care center, parents should consider
the following:

1. a staff of trained, professional people who have worked in their center for
   a prolonged period of time;
2. small groups of children for each counselor or teacher. Government guide-
70   lines recommend a ratio of three to one for infants, four to one for two-
   year-olds, and eight to one for children from three to six;
3. **suitable** games and activities for the child's development;
4. freedom for parents to visit without advance notice.

Attention should be given to these points as well as to the cleanliness, safety,
75 equipment, and nutritional standards of the center.

Children are a nation's most precious natural resource. Naturally, parents want to be confident that their children receive the best of care under the supervision of others. Quality day care does exist and parents do have options. Even though high-quality day care is not currently available to every
80 family, the future looks promising. Government, industry, and religious groups are making serious efforts to provide and upgrade this much-needed service.

A. True/False Statements

After reading the passage for the first time, read the following statements and check whether they are True (T) or False (F).

_____ T _____ F   1. The structure of the typical American family has been changing.

_____ T _____ F   2. The majority of single parents are divorced.

_____ T _____ F   3. Parents never worry about leaving their children with strangers.

_____ T _____ F   4. Psychologists agree on the value of day-care centers for children.

_____ T _____ F   5. All day-care centers do not offer the same high standards.

_____ T _____ F   6. The cost is the most important factor in selecting a day-care center.

_____ T _____ F   7. It is the parents' responsibility to investigate day-care centers carefully.

B. Comprehension Questions

1. The main idea of the article is:
   a. Lifestyles in America are changing and families are developing into new structures.
   b. Day-care centers are becoming an important element in modern American life as more mothers work full-time.
   c. Many children of mothers who work dislike being put into day-care centers.
   d. Because more mothers work, day-care centers are becoming important and need to be selected with care.
2. How has the structure of the American family been changing in recent years?
3. As a result of these changes, what kind of services have become essential?
4. What opposing views do psychologists have about the effects of day-care centers on children?
5. What do psychologists who support the idea of day-care centers say about the positive effects on children?
6. What negative points do psychologists make?
7. Why do parents have to be very careful in selecting a day-care center?
8. What should parents look for when selecting a day-care center?

C. Vocabulary in Context Exercise: Part I

A. Read the sentences below carefully, and try to understand the meaning of the boldface words.
   1. Mary **mistreated** her children badly. She beat them severely, didn't feed them well, and locked them in the basement for hours at a time.

She treated them in such an **abominable** way that they were eventually taken from her and placed in a foster home.

2. When traffic on the main highway become too heavy, John took the first exit and continued on an **alternate** road. The **alternative** got him to work right on time.

3. It was very **astute** of Joanne to figure out a way to fix her television set with only a screwdriver. It works perfectly, and she didn't have to pay to have it repaired.

4. In the United States, health officials have been trying to eliminate measles, a **contagious** childhood illness. If one child in a class becomes sick with measles, all of the children in the same class who haven't already had it will most likely get it too.

5. The people in that part of the country live under **deplorable** conditions. Their houses are made of discarded wood and do not have any plumbing or heating, and there is no garbage pickup in their area.

6. Tom is a **despicable** person. He underpays the people who work for him, then fires them when they complain. He mistreats his wife, ignores his children, and fights with his friends.

7. Joyce is a very **enterprising** woman. She started her own business working from her home, then rented office space, and hired several people to work for her. Within a year she had built up two offices and hired twenty employees.

8. In the United States, the number of cars on the road has **proliferated** throughout the last few decades. It is hard to believe how many more cars there are today compared to the number of cars there were twenty years ago, for example.

B. Match the following words with the definitions and synonyms listed below.

abominable	astute	deplorable	enterprising
alternate (adj.)	contagious	despicable	proliferate
alternative (n.)			

1. _____ : contemptible; meriting hatred

2. _____ : clever

3. _____ : increase significantly

4. _____ : energetic, independent, and willing to experiment

5. _____ : detestable; revolting

6. _____ : communicable by contact

7. _____ : a choice between two or more things or actions

8. _____ : unfortunate; abominable

C. Vocabulary in Context Exercise: Part II

A. Read the sentences below carefully, and try to understand the meaning of the boldface words.

1. The bicycle has **evolved** from a simple two-wheeled device with a seat and handles to a complex machine with gears, brakes, bearings, and assorted extras such as lights and bells.

2. Susan was very **harried** at her job. She worked for three people at the same time. All of them were busy and had important deadlines for the work they asked her to do. In addition, she had to answer the telephone and receive people who came into the office.

3. Once you have had certain diseases such as mumps and chicken pox or had vaccinations for such diseases as smallpox, you develop an **immunity** to these diseases. That is to say, you will never get them again.

4. Harry leads a very **mediocre** existence. He has a steady job that is not interesting. He lives in a quiet part of town that offers no cultural activities. He usually stays home at night and reads a magazine. He talks only about what he's seen on television.

5. In the United States, the social **strata** are mainly based on an individual's income and, to a lesser degree, on his or her job.

6. Monica is, without a doubt, the most **suitable** person for that job. She has the education, the work experience, and the personality to succeed.

7. Dennis does not want to gain any weight. He also does not want to lose weight. Therefore, he is trying to **sustain** his present weight by eating carefully.

8. There has been a significant **turnover** in the population of that neighborhood. In the last five years, most of the elderly people have moved out and been replaced by young working couples. The wealthier people have moved to different parts of the city, and they have also been replaced by young, professional people.

B. Match the following words with the definitions and synonyms listed below.

evolve	immunity	stratum (sing.)	sustain
harried	mediocre	strata (pl.)	turnover
		suitable	

1. _____ : shift; change

2. _____ : levels; divisions

3. _____ : develop gradually

4. _____ : maintain

5. _____ : ability to resist disease

6. _____ : harassed; troubled by problems and anxieties

7. _____ : appropriate; proper

8. _____ : ordinary; of middle quality

D. Detailed Comprehension Exercise

Answer the following questions. Refer back to the passage wherever necessary.

1. Read lines 1–9.

   a. What does **comprised of** mean? _____

   b. What does the expression **breadwinner** mean? _____

   c. What does **for the most part** mean? _____

   d. In line 4, why is the word *family* italicized? _____

   e. What does **nuclear** mean in the term **nuclear family?** _____
   f. In line 8, how does *in other words* connect what follows it to what

      precedes it? _____

2. "These children gave rise to the creation of the term *latchkey children.*" (lines 10–11)

   a. What does **gave rise to** mean? _____

   b. Why is *latchkey children* italicized? _____

3. "The majority of single-parent homes are a consequence of divorce." (lines 12–13)

   What does **consequence** mean? _____

4. "Death of a spouse accounts for another segment of this category." (lines 13–14)

   What does **accounts for** mean? _____

5. "—a new phenomenon appearing on the American scene—" (line 15)

   What does *on the American scene* refer to? _____

6. In line 17, what does **evolution** mean? _____

7. ". . . day care has shifted from being an option of the well-to-do to a necessity among families in all economic strata." (lines 20–21)

   a. What does **shifted** mean? _____

   b. What two words connect the two facts in this sentence? _____

8. ". . . it is not uncommon to find a harried mother . . ." (line 22)

   What is the actual meaning of **not uncommon?** _____

9. "This arrangement is frequently disrupted by personal emergencies on the part of any one of these people. . . ." (lines 23–25)

    a. What does **disrupted** mean? _____

    b. What does **on the part of** mean? _____

10. ". . . a significant number of children are cared for by such unlicensed caretakers as neighbors, relatives, and enterprising people." (lines 26–27)

    a. What does **caretakers** mean? _____

    b. How do the words *such as* connect the term *caretakers* with *neigh-*

    bors, relatives, and enterprising people? _____

11. ". . . many parents have mixed feelings about leaving their children with strangers as opposed to relatives or friends." (lines 29–30)

    What are *mixed feelings?* _____

12. In lines 30–31, what does **adverse** mean? In other words, what kinds of

    effects are adverse effects? _____

13. "Psychologists, too, have expressed conflicting views on the value of day-care experiences for young children." (lines 31–33)

    a. What does *too* refer to? In other words, what phrase could be substi-

    tuted for *too?* _____

    b. To what do the conflicting views correspond? _____

14. "Those who advocate child day care claim that children . . . learn to perform many tasks by themselves. . . ." (lines 33–34)

    a. What does **advocate** mean? _____

    b. How do you know? _____

15. In line 35, what does *in addition* refer to? _____

16. "When it is time to start elementary school, they adjust more readily." (lines 38–39)

    What does **readily** mean? _____

17. "On the other hand, dissenting psychologists claim that children in poor or mediocre day-care situations are definitely disadvantaged." (lines 40–41)

    a. How does *on the other hand* connect paragraph three with paragraph

    four? _____

    b. What does **dissenting** mean? _____

    c. How do you know? _____

18. "In centers where the ratio of children to teachers is very high, children

invariably get inadequate attention. Furthermore . . ." (lines 41–43)

  a. From the context, and by word analysis, what does **invariably** mean?

_____

  b. How does *furthermore* relate the sentence before with what follows?

_____

19. "This inconsistency in caretakers upsets very young children." (lines 44–45)

What does *this inconsistency in caretakers* refer to? _____
20. "All doctors, psychologists, and laymen. . . ." (line 45)

What are **laymen?** _____

21. What does **ever-changing** in line 47 mean? _____
22. ". . . children in day-care centers come down with contagious ailments frequently." (lines 48–49)

What does **come down with** mean? _____
23. "Dissenters claim that high sanitary standards . . . can keep these problems to a minimum." (lines 49–50)

What are the *dissenters*? _____
24. "Indeed, exposure to other children helps youngsters build up immunity to disease before they attend elementary school." (lines 50–52)

  a. What does **indeed** mean? _____

  b. How does it relate what precedes it to what follows it? _____
25. "These objections to day-care centers are valid in some instances; and in fact, not all centers are acceptable places in which to entrust children." (lines 53–54)

  a. What does *in some instances* refer to? _____

_____

  b. How does *in fact* relate what follows it to what precedes it?

_____

  c. What does **entrust** mean? _____
26. "Day-care centers range from being excellent to mediocre to deplorable." (lines 54–55)

What does *range from . . . to* indicate? _____
27. "It is up to the parents to investigate centers, interview the management, and observe the personnel." (lines 60–61)

Who are the **personnel?** _____

28. What does **well-being** in line 64 mean? _____

29. "When assessing a child-care center, . . ." (line 65)

    What does **assessing** mean? _____

30. "Government guidelines recommend a ratio of three to one for infants. . . ." (lines 69–70)

    What does **ratio** mean? _____

31. "Quality day care does exist and parents do have options."(lines 78–79) Why are the verbs written in this manner, that is, with their auxiliaries?

    _____

32. "Even though high-quality day care is not currently available to every family, the future looks promising." (lines 79–80)

    a. What does *even though* introduce? _____

    b. What does **promising** mean? _____

33. What does **upgrade** mean in line 81? _____

    _____

E. Vocabulary in Context Quiz

Complete each blank space with a synonym of the word(s) in parentheses. You may need to use more than one word.

In years past, a typical American family consisted of a father who was

the (1) _____, a mother who took care of the children and the
        (primary wage-earner)

home, and the children themselves. With the passing of time, the concept of

family has (2) _____ into new kinds of family units. These
        (developed)

units are, for the most part, composed of single parents living with their chil-

dren. Almost all single parents are compelled to work in order to support

their families. It is also a fact that both parents in many traditional families

work. The number of working mothers has (3) _____ in re-
                            (increased significantly)

cent years. As a result, day care for children has changed from a(n)

(4) _____ to a necessity among families in all economic
        (choice)

(5) _____ .
        (levels)

    Psychologists have (6) _____ views on the benefits of
                            (opposing)

day care. Those who (7) _____ (support) day-care centers believe that language development and social skills develop more rapidly and that day-care children adjust more easily to elementary school demands. (8) _____ (Disagreeing) psychologists, however, claim that (9) _____ (ordinary) day care is disadvantageous to children. Frequent (10) _____ (change) in staff and inadequate attention are very undesirable circumstances for children. (11) _____ (Lack of continuity) in caretakers is upsetting to them. Doctors have observed that children in day-care centers contract (12) _____ (communicable) diseases from one another.

It is true that not all day-care centers are run with high standards. In rare cases, some centers are (13)_____ (contemptible) places where children are sexually abused. (14) _____ (Clever) parents carefully (15) _____ (evaluate) several centers before making a choice. Points to investigate include: staff members employed at the center for a(n) (16) _____ (extended) period of time; a small ratio of children to teachers; appropriate activities; freedom for parents to visit without advance notice. Of course, affordability is an important consideration, but it should not be the *only* one. Selecting a(n) (17) _____ (appropriate) center for the child is very comforting to the parents. Although the quality varies from center to center, government and industry are gradually providing more day-care service as well as (18) _____ (improving) it. The future for youngsters in day-care centers looks (19) _____ (hopeful). Some current (20) _____ (opponents) may, perhaps, change their minds about day-care centers.

F. Topics for Discussion and Composition

1. Compare the benefits of having a caretaker at home for young children as opposed to placing them in a day-care center.
2. How may a parent cope with a child who does not adapt well to being in a day-care center?
3. When would a day-care center be advisable for children even though their mothers stay at home?

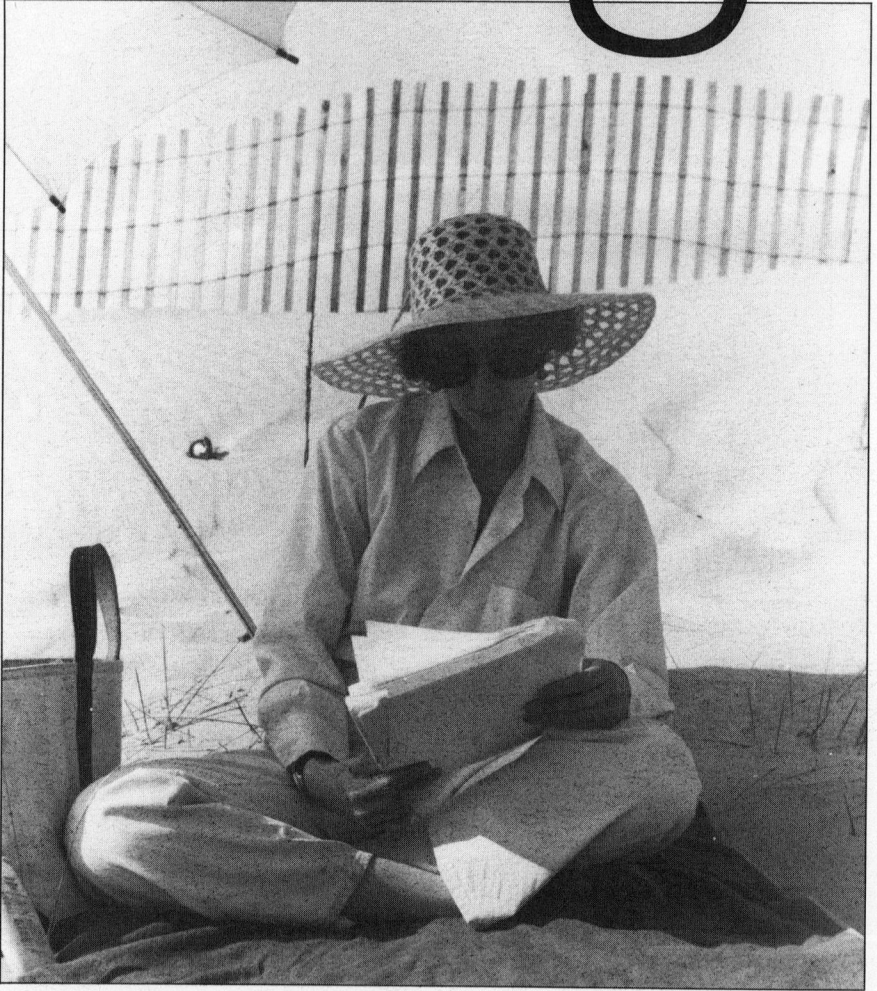

Saving Face

Introductory Questions

1. In your country, how concerned are people with their appearance as they grow older? How concerned are they with maintaining a youthful appearance?
2. Many Americans are very concerned about staying young-looking. How do you think this attitude affects their behavior as they grow older?
3. How much influence do you think advertising has on the way people feel about aging and their appearance?

Saving Face

Although lines in the face are supposedly indications of experience and **wisdom,** many people go to great lengths to **forestall** the inevitable: wrinkles! Lines in facial skin are visible signs of the aging process, and youth-worshiping Americans **tenaciously resist** those telling lines.

5   While most people do not think of the skin as an organ of the body, not only is it really an organ, but it is the largest and the most visible one. It is quite a remarkable one at that. The skin is composed of countless sensory cells, blood vessels, glands, and hair. The functions of the skin are diverse: it protects internal organs, **regulates** body temperature, and conveys external

10 stimuli through nerve endings. The most exposed part of the skin is on the face, and it is this area that most people are concerned about.

    In the youth-oriented, the **ceaseless** effort to keep skin smooth and wrinkle-free has fostered the **boundless** growth of the **cosmetics** industries and professions. There is a never-ending collection of lotions, creams, cleansers,

15 and moisturizers **emanating from** laboratories—all in an effort to **defy** nature. Americans spend staggering sums of money on these products—billions of dollars annually. Plastic surgeons enjoy a **lucrative** business performing cosmetic surgery.

    The aging process of the skin is related to several factors, the first of

20 which is heredity. Obviously, it is impossible to **alter** this factor. Oil glands, which **secrete** oil that lubricates the skin, slow down their output in the mature adult. This decrease in skin oil causes the skin to become drier and the pores to become larger. Some external factors that are detrimental to maintaining smooth, attractive skin are sun, wind, alcohol, smoking, and frequent

25 weight changes. Of all these negative influences, the ultraviolet rays of the sun, the rays that are invisible to the naked eye, are the most damaging.

    Large numbers of people enjoy such outdoor sports as swimming, tennis, jogging, and skiing. Being in the sun causes the skin to change color—a protective response to the burning rays of the sun. The color may change

30 from pink or red to tan or brown, depending on the amount of exposure. Many people regard these skin color changes as **flattering.** Doctors, however, warn that the sun's ultraviolet radiation alters the skin in unhealthy ways. The effects of radiation on the body are **cumulative,** and every day spent in the sun can be harmful. Suntans and sunburns cause the breakdown of the skin's
35 proteins that give the skin its good tone. The erosion of these proteins causes skin to **sag,** brown spots to appear, and tumors to form. Doctors have linked frequent and prolonged exposure to sun with skin cancer. Sunscreen lotion, a relatively new product, effectively blocks out the sun's harmful ultraviolet radiation. Sunscreen lotion is useful when used on all parts of the body that
40 are exposed to the sun.

In spite of the enormous amount of ongoing research in modern laboratories, the most practical program for good skin is equally sensible for general good health.

1. Avoid being in direct sunlight for prolonged periods of time.
45 2. Use sunscreen on all exposed parts of the body.
3. Wear a hat and light-weight long-sleeved shirt outside.
4. Maintain good health via
   a. a nutritious, well-balanced diet.
   b. plenty of water.
50   c. sufficient sleep.
   d. regular exercise.
5. Avoid excessive weight gains and losses.
6. Do not smoke.

7. Use alcohol in moderation.
55 8. Clean and moisturize the skin daily.

In **reflecting** on the matter of wrinkles, is it not better simply to accept them, rather than spend time and money in a vain attempt to remain youthful?

A. True/False Statements

After reading the passage for the first time, read the following statements and check whether they are True (T) or False (F).

_____ T _____ F 1. The skin is the largest organ of the body, and it has many important functions.

_____ T _____ F 2. Men as well as women spend enormous sums of money to look young.

_____ T _____ F 3. Alcohol is the most detrimental factor in the aging of the skin.

_____ T _____ F 4. Ultraviolet rays of the sun can be harmful to the skin.

_____ T _____ F 5. Doctors have proved that exposure to the sun causes skin cancer.

_____ T _____ F 6. Sunscreen lotion does not effectively block out the sun's ultraviolet rays.

B. Comprehension Questions

1. The main idea of the article is:
   a. Because Americans spend so much time on outdoor sports, they damage their skin through overexposure to the sun.
   b. Americans are very much concerned about keeping their appearance youthful.
   c. Plastic surgeons claim that everyone can look younger through cosmetic surgery.
   d. While Americans spend considerable sums of money to maintain a youthful appearance, they also damage their skin through overexposure to the sun.
2. How do Americans feel about getting wrinkles?
3. What is the skin composed of?
4. What functions does the skin perform?
5. What do Americans do to try to keep their skin smooth and youthful?
6. What factors affect the aging process of the skin?
7. How do ultraviolet rays alter the skin?

8. What is an effective means of protecting skin from ultraviolet radiation?
9. How can skin be kept in good condition?

C. Vocabulary in Context Exercise: Part I

A. Read the sentences below carefully, and try to understand the meaning of the boldface words.
   1. After Harold suffered a heart attack, he had to **alter** his lifestyle. Instead of sitting all day, he had to begin walking every day. He also began eating more fruit and vegetables and less red meat. In addition, he stopped smoking. He now lives a very different life.
   2. Children always seem to have **boundless** energy. They play all day without tiring or losing their enthusiasm for what they are doing.
   3. The soldiers set up a **ceaseless** watch over the border to prevent the enemy from crossing into their territory. It was a twenty-four-hour-a-day job.
   4. Most people appreciate the **cosmetic** effect of makeup and attractive clothes.
   5. Cigarette smoke has a harmful, **cumulative** effect on the lungs. In other words, each cigarette smoked adds to the damage done by each preceding cigarette.
   6. When John demanded the ball from Tom, Tom said, "I won't give it to you. Try to take it from me if you can." Because Tom **defied** him, John gave up and walked away.
   7. In many deserts, water **emanates from** underground sources. You need only dig a hole to find it.
   8. Bessie has very light skin, so red is a very **flattering** color for her. It reflects a soft red color onto her face, which is very attractive.
   9. Joanne was a very poor worker. She was never on time and rarely did her work effectively, so she knew she was going to lose her job. She tried to **forestall** being fired by working hard on Thursday, but it was too late to perform well. Her boss fired her on Friday.

B. Match the following words with the definitions and synonyms listed below.

alter	ceaseless	cumulative	emanate from	forestall
boundless	cosmetic	defy	flattering	

1. _____ : come out from a source; spring from

2. _____ : change

3. _____ : prevent; obstruct

4. _____ : challenge; confront

5. _____ : immeasurable; unlimited

6. _____ : increasing by additions without a corresponding loss

7. _____ : setting off to advantage; displaying something favorably

8. _____ : beautifying

9. _____ : constant; continual

C. Vocabulary in Context Exercise: Part II

A. Read the sentences below carefully, and try to understand the meaning of the boldface words.
   1. Natalie has a very **lucrative** part-time job. She buys sweaters directly from a manufacturer, then takes them to her office. She buys them for five dollars and sells them to her co-workers for ten dollars, making a 100 percent profit.
   2. After a successful interview, Dennis was offered a very demanding job. He **reflected** on the advantages and disadvantages of the job for a few days, then called the company back and accepted.
   3. In most countries, the taxes that people pay are **regulated** by law. People pay a certain percentage of their income, and they also pay a certain percentage of tax on merchandise they buy.
   4. When you are in good health generally, your body is able to **resist** many disease-causing bacteria and viruses. When you are not feeling healthy, you are more likely to become sick.
   5. Yolanda had a beautiful wool sweater, which she hung on a hanger in the closet for a few weeks. When she took it out, she saw that it had stretched in the shoulders and had begun to **sag.**
   6. Many people are sensitive to the odor of onions, and whenever they cut onions, the people's eyes **secrete** tears.
   7. A thief came into the house while everyone was sleeping. Fortunately, the family's dog heard him and attacked him, biting him on the leg. Although the thief hit the dog and tried to shake it off, the dog held on **tenaciously** until the family woke up and called the police.
   8. Many people go to school and study hard to learn a great deal of information, but **wisdom** is a type of knowledge that cannot be learned in any school.
B. Match the following words with the definitions and synonyms listed below.

   lucrative   regulate   sag   tenaciously
   reflect   resist   secrete   wisdom

   1. _____ : persistently; stubbornly

2. _____ : sink from a normal position; droop

3. _____ : insight; good sense

4. _____ : profitable

5. _____ : fight off; oppose

6. _____ : reconsider; think quietly and calmly

7. _____ : govern; fix the time, amount, rate, or degree of something

8. _____ : produce and emit; form and give off

D. Detailed Comprehension Exercise

Answer the following questions. Refer back to the passage wherever necessary.

1. "Although lines in the face are supposedly indications of experience and wisdom, many people go to great lengths to forestall the inevitable: wrinkles!" (lines 1–2)

   a. What does **supposedly** mean? _____

   b. What does **go to great lengths** mean? _____

   c. What are **wrinkles**? _____

   d. How do you know? _____

2. "Lines in facial skin are visible signs of the aging process, and youth-worshiping Americans tenaciously resist those telling lines." (lines 3–4)

   What does **youth-worshiping** mean? _____

3. "While most people do not think of the skin as an organ of the body, not only is it really an organ, but it is also the largest and the most visible one. It is quite a remarkable one at that." (lines 5–7)

   a. What does *while* introduce? _____

   b. How do *not only* and *but also* connect the two thoughts in the

      sentence? _____

   c. How does *at that* relate to the rest of the sentence? _____

4. "The skin is composed of countless sensory cells, . . ." (lines 7–8)

   What does **countless** mean? _____

5. "In the youth-oriented, the ceaseless effort to keep skin smooth and wrinkle-free has fostered the boundless growth of the cosmetics industries and professions." (lines 12–14)

a. What does **youth-oriented** mean? _____

b. What does **wrinkle-free** mean? _____

c. How do you know? _____

6. "Plastic surgeons enjoy a lucrative business performing cosmetic surgery." (lines 17–18)
   What is the relationship between the words *surgeon* and *surgery?*

   _____

7. "The aging process of the skin is related to several factors, the first of which is heredity. Obviously, it is impossible to alter this factor." (lines 19–20)

   a. What does *which* refer to? _____

   b. What does *this factor* refer to? _____

8. "Oil glands, which secrete oil that lubricates the skin, slow down their output in the mature adult. This decrease in skin oil causes the skin to become drier. . . ." (lines 20–22)

   a. What does **lubricate** mean? _____

   b. How do you know? _____

   c. What does **output** mean? _____

   d. How do you know? _____

9. "Of all these negative influences, the ultraviolet rays of the sun, the rays that are invisible to the naked eye, are the most damaging." (lines 25–26)

   What does **to the naked eye** mean? _____

10. "Large numbers of people enjoy such outdoor sports as swimming, tennis, jogging, and skiing." (lines 27–28)

    How does *such as* relate *outdoor sports* to what follows? _____

11. "The color may change from pink or red to tan or brown, depending on the amount of exposure." (lines 29–30)

    What does **depending on** mean? _____

12. "Many people regard these skin color changes as flattering. Doctors, however, warn that the sun's ultraviolet radiation alters the skin in unhealthy ways." (lines 31–32)

    a. Does the opinion of doctors differ from the opinion of many people

    with regard to changing the color of the skin? _____

    b. How do you know? _____

13. "Suntans and sunburns cause the breakdown of the skin's proteins that

give the skin its good tone. The erosion of these proteins causes skin to sag. . . . Doctors have linked frequent and prolonged exposure to sun with skin cancer." (lines 34–37)

a. What does **breakdown** mean? _____

b. What does **erosion** mean? _____

c. How do you know? _____

d. What does **prolonged** mean? _____

e. How do you know? _____

14. "In spite of the enormous amount of ongoing research in modern laboratories, the most practical program for good skin care is equally sensible for general good health." (lines 41–43)

a. What does *in spite of* introduce? _____

b. What does **ongoing** mean? _____

c. How do you know? _____

d. What does *equally sensible* refer to? _____

15. "Maintain good health via a nutritious, well-balanced diet." (lines 47–48)

What is a **well-balanced** diet? _____

_____

E. Vocabulary in Context Quiz

Complete each blank space with a synonym of the word(s) in parentheses. You may need to use more than one word.

Lines on the face are usually signs of life experience and

(1) _____ ; but to many people they are nothing more than
    (good sense)

horrible wrinkles! Some people would try almost anything to

(2) _____ this visible, psychologically painful sign of aging.
    (prevent)

This intense desire to maintain wrinkle-free skin has generated the

(3) _____ growth of the cosmetics industry and professions.
    (unlimited)

Chemists (4) _____ produce cleansers, lotions, moisturizers,
    (continually)

and powders in modern laboratories for the purpose of keeping skin soft and

smooth forever—in other words, (5) _____ the natural aging
                                        (challenging)
process. Men as well as women spend incredible sums of money in their

efforts to (6) _____ the aging process. The business of beauty
                    (fight off)
is   a   (7) _____   one.   Some   people   are   so
                  (profitable)
(8) _____ in keeping the youthful look that they have doctors
         (persistent)
perform plastic surgery for purely (9) _____ reasons.
                                              (beautifying)
   The skin is actually the largest and the most visible organ of the body,

and it has a few important functions. It protects internal organs,

(10) _____ body temperature, and conveys external stimuli
           (governs)
through nerve endings.

   People are most concerned with keeping facial skin wrinkle-free. This is

not always an easy task because the condition of the skin is related to several

factors.   The   first   is   heredity,   which   is   impossible   to

(11) _____. The skin is partly composed of glands that
           (change)
(12) _____ oil that (13) _____ the skin. As the
        (produce and emit)   (oils)
adult matures, this secretion diminishes, creating dry skin and large pores.

Other factors that make faces less than flattering are sun, wind, alcohol, smok-

ing, and frequent weight changes. The most damaging factor is the ultraviolet

radiation from the sun. The effects of radiation on the body are

(14) _____ ; (15) _____ exposure causes the
        (increased by additions)   (continued)
(16) _____ of the skin's proteins and makes the skin
          (destruction)
(17) _____.
           (droop)
   In spite of (18) _____ research, the most practical pro-
                          (growing)
gram for good skin care is (19) _____ sensible for general
                                        (uniformly)
good health. Looking good and feeling good will (20) _____
                                                              (spring)
from following such a plan.

F. Topics for Discussion and Composition

1. How do you weigh the flattering effects of a suntan against the increased risk of skin disease?
2. What are the advantages of striving to maintain a youthful appearance?
3. What are the disadvantages of striving to maintain a youthful appearance?
4. What do you think is a sensible way to take care of skin without using drastic measures such as cosmetic surgery?

9

The Value of Friendship

Introductory Questions

1. There is a saying in English: "A joy shared is a joy multiplied." What is the meaning behind this saying?
2. What do you look for in choosing people for friends? Why?
3. What is the difference between an acquaintance and a close friend? Why do we need both in our lives?
4. What makes friendship grow? Conversely, what destroys friendships?

The Value of Friendship

Friendship is both a source of pleasure and a component of good health. People who have close friends naturally enjoy their company. Of equal importance are the concrete emotional benefits they **derive.** When something sensational happens to us, sharing the happiness of the occasion with friends
5 **intensifies** our joy. Conversely, in times of trouble and tension, when our spirits are low, **unburdening** our worries and fears to **compassionate** friends alleviates the stress. Moreover, we may even get some practical suggestions for solving a particular problem.

From time to time, we are insensitive and behave in a way that hurts
10 someone's feelings. Afterward, when we feel guilty and down in the dumps, friends can reassure us. This positive interaction is **therapeutic,** and much less expensive than visits to a psychologist.

Adolescence and old age are the two stages in our lives when the need for friendship is crucial. In the former stage, teens are **plagued** by uncertainty
15 and mixed feelings. In the latter stage, older people are upset by feelings of uselessness and insignificance. In both instances, friends can make a dramatic difference. With close friends in their lives, people develop courage and positive attitudes. Teenagers have the moral support to assert their individuality; the elderly approach their advanced years with optimism and an interest in
20 life. These positive outlooks are vital to cope successfully with the crises **inherent** in these two stages of life.

Throughout life, we rely on small groups of people for love, admiration, respect, moral support, and help. Almost everyone has a "network" of friends: co-workers, neighbors, and schoolmates. While both men and women have
25 such friends, evidence is accumulating that indicates men rarely make close friends. Men are sociable and frequently have numerous business acquaintances, golf buddies, and so on. However, friendship does not merely involve a sharing of activities; it is a sharing of self on a very personal level. Customarily, men have shied away from close relationships in which they confide in

94

30 others. By bottling up their emotions, men deprive themselves of a healthy
outlet for their negative feelings.

The picture is different among middle-class, middle-aged women. They
tend to be more emotionally stable in times of personal **turmoil** because they
vent feelings and concerns. They receive support and sympathy from close
35 friends. In fact, being **adept** at forming close friendships is a most valuable
asset for widows. Having a few good friends makes the transition from living
with a husband to living alone less lonely and frightening. Conversely, widowers whose sole confidants were their wives, have greater difficulty adjusting, feel abandoned, and deteriorate physically more rapidly.

40 Because friendships **enhance** our lives, it is important to cultivate them.
Unfortunately, it is somewhat difficult to make long-lasting close friends. People are mobile, and mobility puts a strain on friendships. Long distances between friends discourage intimacy. Long-distance telephone conversations are
costly, and letter writing is not a deeply ingrained habit. Divorce is also de-
45 structive to friendships. In many cases, when divorce occurs, friendships **disintegrate** because couples usually prefer to associate with other couples.

People choose some friends because they are fun to be with; they "make
things happen." Likewise, common interests appear to be a significant factor
in selecting friends. Families with children, for instance, tend to gravitate
50 toward families with children. It is normal to befriend people who have similar lifestyles, and organizations such as Parents Without Partners have appeared on the scene as a natural outgrowth of this tendency. These groups
provide an opportunity to socialize, make new acquaintances and friends, ob-
tain helpful advice in adapting smoothly to a new lifestyle. Other groups focus
55 on a specific interest such as camping or politics. It is perfectly acceptable to

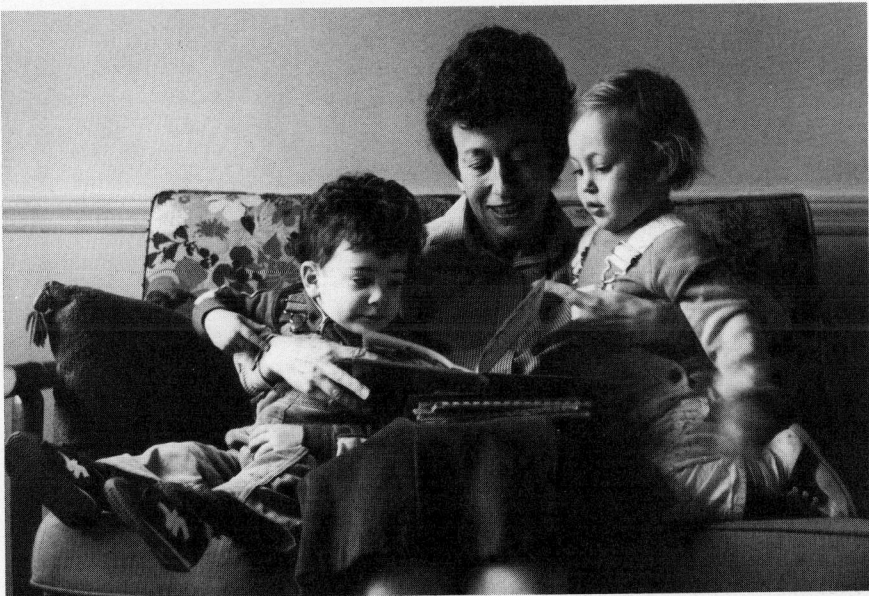

select friends for special qualities as long as there is a balanced giving and
taking that is **mutually** satisfying.

60 Very close and trusted friends share confidences candidly. They feel secure that they will not be ridiculed or derided, and their confidences will be
honored. Betraying a trust is a very quick and painful way to terminate a
friendship.

As friendships solidify, ties strengthen. Intimate relationships enrich
people's lives. Some components of a thriving friendship are honesty, natu-
ralness, thoughtfulness, some common interests.

65 Circumstances and people are constantly changing. Some friendships
last "forever"; others do not. Nevertheless, friendship is an essential ingredi-
ent in the making of a healthful, rewarding life.

A. True/False Statements

After reading the passage for the first time, read the following statements and
check whether they are True (T) or False (F).

_____ T _____ F 1. When a person feels depressed, a friend can be of help.

_____ T _____ F 2. Adolescents as well as elderly people have a compelling
need for friends.

_____ T _____ F 3. Men make close friends as readily as women.

_____ T _____ F 4. Friendship always means sharing activities.

_____ T _____ F 5. Because our society is mobile, we pick up more close
friends.

B. Comprehension Questions

1. The main idea of the article is:
   a. A good friend always helps another friend in times of trouble.
   b. Friends are essential in our lives because of the emotional benefits they
      provide.
   c. We all have friends at every stage in our lives.
   d. A good friend will always lend you money when you need it.
2. How can friends help us in times of trouble?
3. Why is the support of good friends so essential to adolescents?
4. Why is the support of good friends so essential to older people?
5. What do we mean by a network of friends?
6. Why do many women tend to be more emotionally stable in times of personal crisis?
7. Why is it difficult to maintain close friends over the years?

8. Regardless of the reasons we choose friends, what quality must exist in each relationship?

C. Vocabulary in Context Exercise: Part I

A. Read the sentences below carefully, and try to understand the meaning of the boldface words.
   1. Michael was very slow when he began typing and made many mistakes. He practiced for two hours every day and after a few months he became **adept** at typing quickly and accurately.
   2. Monica is a very **compassionate** woman. She always takes time to listen to her friends when they have problems. Furthermore, she is always ready with kind words and good advice.
   3. Susan is usually calm, but this week she feels very anxious. Her anxiety **derives** from the fact that she has to take an important exam on Friday.
   4. If you have trouble swallowing a pill such as aspirin, put the aspirin into a glass of water. The aspirin will **disintegrate,** and you will be able to drink it easily.
   5. While the use of too much salt is unhealthful, the careful use of small amounts of salt actually **enhances** the flavor of food.
   6. One of the problems **inherent** in having children is deciding how to educate them.
   7. If you want to **intensify** the light in this room, change the 50-watt bulb for a 200-watt bulb. Then you will have a very bright light.
B. Match the following words with the definitions and synonyms listed below.

adept	derive	enhance	intensify
compassionate	disintegrate	inherent	

   1. _____ : originate; stem

   2. _____ : strengthen; deepen

   3. _____ : increase; heighten

   4. _____ : expert

   5. _____ : belonging by nature; intrinsic

   6. _____ : sympathetic

   7. _____ : break apart; deteriorate

C. Vocabulary in Context Exercise: Part II

A. Read the sentences on page 98 carefully, and try to understand the meaning of the boldface words.

1. Tom and Harry take turns driving to work. On Monday and Tuesday, Tom drives to work and takes Harry with him. On Wednesday and Thursday, Harry drives to work and takes Tom with him. This system is of **mutual** benefit to them; that is, it is an advantage to both Harry *and* Tom.

2. Ann has been **plagued** by doubt every since she accepted a new, more responsible job. She is worried that she doesn't have enough experience; she is afraid that her office staff won't accept her authority; and she is fearful that she won't be able to meet deadlines, or time limits, on her work.

3. Whenever Dorothy feels depressed, she always goes to the pool for a swim. The exercise and warm water leave her feeling happier and refreshed. Swimming is a **therapeutic** activity for her.

4. When Harold's parents decided to move to another city, Harold's feelings were in a **turmoil.** He was excited by the idea of living in a new city, but he felt very sad at losing his old friends. In addition, he loved the school he was attending, and was frightened by the idea of having to meet new classmates and adjust to a new school. As a result, he had very mixed feelings about leaving. One moment he was happy, and the next moment he felt like crying.

5. When Debbie lost her job, she felt very depressed, but she couldn't speak to anyone at work. When she went home, however, she called her best friend and **unburdened** her feelings. When she told her friend how unhappy she was, Debbie began to feel better.

6. When Caroline feels very angry, she doesn't keep her emotions hidden. She **vents** her anger by shouting at an imaginary person. When she feels less angry, she talks over her feelings with her friends.

B. Match the following words with the definitions and synonyms listed below.

mutual	therapeutic	unburden
plague	turmoil	vent

1. _____ : relieve or release by expressing

2. _____ : shared in common

3. _____ : to give vigorous or emotional expression to

4. _____ : remedial; something that cures

5. _____ : trouble; bother

6. _____ : an extremely confused or upset condition

D. Detailed Comprehension Exercise

Answer the following questions. Refer back to the passage wherever necessary.

1. "Friendship is both a source of pleasure and a component of good health." (line 1)

   What does **component** mean? _____

2. "People who have close friends naturally enjoy their company. Of equal importance are the concrete emotional benefits they derive." (lines 1–3)

   What is of equal importance with concrete emotional benefits? _____

3. "When something sensational happens to us, sharing the happiness of the occasion with friends intensifies our joy. Conversely, in times of trouble and tension, when our spirits are low, unburdening our worries and fears to compassionate friends alleviates the stress." (lines 3–7)

   a. How does *conversely* relate what precedes it to what follows it?

   _____

   b. What does **alleviate** mean? _____

4. " . . . when our spirits are low, unburdening our worries and fears to compassionate friends alleviates the stress. Moreover, we may even get some practical suggestions for solving a particular problem." (lines 5–8)

   How does *moreover* relate what precedes it to what follows it? _____

5. "From time to time, we are insensitive and behave in a way that hurts someone's feelings. Afterward, when we feel guilty and down in the dumps, friends can reassure us." (lines 9–11)

   a. What does **from time to time** mean? _____

   b. What does **down in the dumps** mean? _____

6. "Adolescence and old age are the two stages in our lives when the need for friendship is crucial. In the former stage, teens are plagued by uncertainty and mixed feelings. In the latter stage, older people are upset by feelings of uselessness and insignificance." (lines 13–16)

   a. What age are *adolescents?* _____

   b. How do you know? That is, what word in lines 13–16 is a synonym of

   adolescents? _____

   c. What stage does the *former stage* refer to? _____

   d. What stage does the *latter stage* refer to? _____

   e. What does **former** mean? _____

   f. What does **latter** mean? _____

7. "In both instances, friends can make a dramatic difference." (lines 16–17)

   What does *both instances* refer to? _____

   _____

8. "With close friends in their lives, people develop courage and positive attitudes. Teenagers have the moral support to assert their individuality; the elderly approach their advanced years with optimism and an interest in life. These positive outlooks are vital to cope successfully. . . . " (lines 17–20)

What are *these positive outlooks?* _____

_____

9. "Almost everyone has a 'network' of friends: co-workers, neighbors, and schoolmates." (lines 23–24)

a. Why is *network* in quotation marks? _____

b. What does **network** mean in this context? _____

10. "Customarily, men have shied away from close relationships in which they confide in others. By bottling up their emotions, men deprive themselves of a natural outlet for their negative feelings." (lines 28–31)

a. What does **customarily** mean? _____

b. What does **shy away from** mean? _____

c. What does **bottle up** mean? _____

11. "The picture is different among middle-class, middle-aged women." (line 32)

a. What do you think *middle class* refers to? _____

b. How old are *middle-aged* women? _____

12. "Having a few good friends makes the transition from living with a husband to living alone less lonely and frightening. Conversely, widowers whose sole confidants were their wives, have greater difficulty adjusting. . . . " (lines 36–39)

a. What does **transition from . . . to . . .** mean? _____

b. How does *conversely* relate what follows it to what precedes it?

_____

c. What is a **widower?** _____

d. What is a **widow?** _____

e. What does **sole** mean? _____

13. " . . . it is somewhat difficult to make long-lasting close friends. People are mobile, and mobility puts a strain on friendships. Long distances between friends discourage intimacy." (lines 41–43)

a. What does **long-lasting** mean? _____

b. What does **strain** mean? _____

14. "Divorce is also destructive to friendships. In many cases, when divorce occurs, friendships disintegrate because couples usually prefer to associate with other couples." (lines 44–46)
How does the second sentence relate to the first sentence?

_____

15. "People choose some friends because they are fun to be with; they 'make things happen.' Likewise, common interests appear to be a significant factor in selecting friends." (lines 47–49)

a. Why is *make things happen* in quotation marks? _____

b. What does **to make things happen** mean? _____

c. How does *likewise* relate what follows it to what precedes it?

In other words, what does **likewise** mean? _____

16. "Families with children, for instance, tend to gravitate toward families with children." (lines 49–50)

a. What does **for instance** mean? _____

b. What is the idea of this sentence an instance of? _____

17. "It is normal to befriend people who have similar lifestyles, and organizations such as Parents Without Partners have appeared on the scene as a natural outgrowth of this tendency." (lines 50–52)

a. What does **befriend** mean? _____

b. What does **outgrowth** mean? _____

18. "It is perfectly acceptable to select friends for special qualities as long as there is a balanced giving and taking that is mutually satisfying." (lines 55–57)

a. What does **as long as** mean? _____

b. What does **a balanced giving and taking** mean? _____

19. "Very close and trusted friends share confidences candidly. They feel secure that they will not be ridiculed or derided, and their confidences will be honored. Betraying a trust is a very quick and painful way to terminate a friendship." (lines 58–61)

What does **betraying a trust** mean? _____

20. "Some friendships last 'forever'; others do not."

a. Why is *forever* in quotation marks? _____

b. What does **forever** mean in this context? _____

E. Vocabulary in Context Quiz

Complete each blank space with a synonym of the word(s) in parentheses.
You may need to use more than one word.

Friendship is valuable for two reasons: It is a source of pleasure as well

as a(n) (1)_____ of good health. Pleasure and happy feelings
                (part)
are (2) _____ when shared with friends. Special celebrations
            (deepened)
become fond memories when friends are part of these events. On the other

hand, when we face problems and feel (3) _____ by them,
                                            (bothered)
friends can be helpful. When (4) _____ friends allow us to
                                    (sympathetic)
(5) _____ our fears, our stress is reduced. At times when we
            (relieve)
feel (6) _____ about mistreating someone, friends can be re-
            (depressed)
assuring. All this positive interaction provides concrete emotional benefits

that (7) _____ from friendship. In many ways, friendship is
                (stem)
actually (8) _____. During (9) _____ and old
                (remedial)   (the teen years)
age, friends are an important source of reassurance and positive feelings about

ourselves.

Men do not form close friendships as easily as women. Rather, they

have many acquaintances. They tend to share activities more than "self." Of-

ten, a man's (10) _____ confidant is his wife. Women
                    (only)
(11) _____ their concerns more readily and are generally
            (release)
more (12) _____ at building close friendships. This trait is a
            (expert)
great asset for (13) _____ , and at other times when life is in
                    (women whose husbands have died)
(14) _____ .
        (a confused state)
Although friendships (15)_____ our lives, we don't keep
                            (heighten)
all friends for a lifetime. High mobility in American life is a factor that both

promotes new friendships and (16) _____ old ones. People
                                    (breaks apart)

are attracted to others with (17) _____ interests. Interests
                                          (shared)
change at various times in life, and friends do too. Often, however, people

have just a few lifelong friends. Confidences are shared candidly with these

people without any fear of being ridiculed. We benefit from trusting friend-

ships with others. (18) _____, others enjoy the same
                               (In the same way)
(19) _____ from us. To (20) _____ a trust
              (advantages)   (violate)
would destroy a friendship. Without a doubt, friendships are essential for a

full, happy, healthful life.

F. Topics for Discussion and Composition

1. There is a proverb that says: "A friend in need is a friend indeed." Discuss
   an incident when this was true for you.
2. When you are struggling with a setback or anxiety, how do you cope? Do
   you (a) keep it to yourself; (b) discuss it with a friend; or (c) go to a doctor?
   What are the advantages and disadvantages of each option?
3. How can a teenager's choice of friends influence his or her life?
4. How is friendship therapeutic?

10

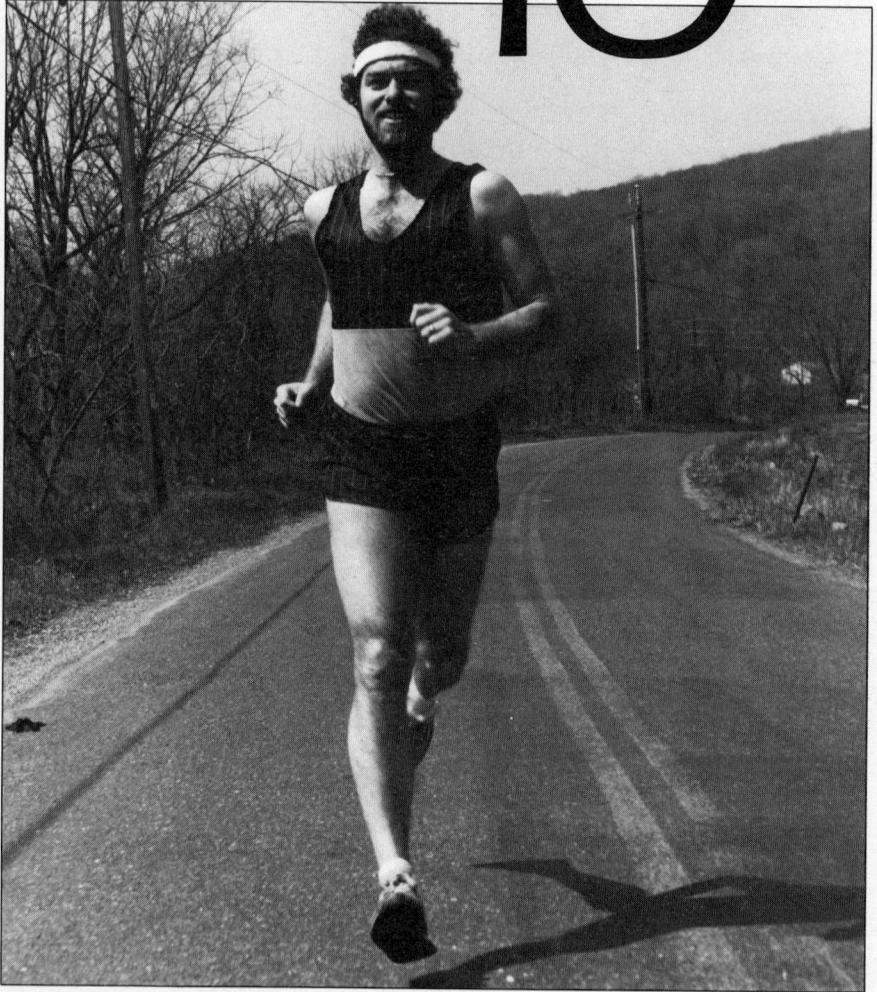

The Fitness Craze

Introductory Questions

1. Good health has come to mean more than simply the absence of illness. What else does good health mean?
2. What are some principles of good health in the areas of nutrition, physical exercise, and mental attitude?
3. How is it possible to overdo these principles?
4. Under what circumstances should employers take responsibility for maintaining the health of their employees?

The Fitness Craze

Back in the sixteenth century, Ponce de Leon stirred up a great deal of hope when he proclaimed that he had discovered the Fountain of Youth in Florida. People were **ecstatic** at the idea of being young forever. Being young has universal appeal. Even today, in the last segment of the twentieth century,
5 people are searching for the qualities that youth **encompasses:** good health, mental alertness, physical attractiveness, and **vigor**—in a word, fitness. Fitness is the magical term that has **pervaded** our daily lives. Via the media, we are constantly bombarded with suggestions to be slim, do exercise, and feel fit. Many television and radio programs are devoted to fitness information and
10 group exercise. Newspapers and magazines regularly feature columns that present the latest nutritional discoveries and exercise equipment. In fact, it is almost impossible to pick up a general interest magazine and not find the perfect diet and easy exercise programs. Every monthly issue invariably features new **versions** of the same theme. Countless books and tapes on fitness
15 are available in bookstores and libraries. The medical profession, too, advocates being slender, doing exercise, and feeling energetic. **Adhering to** these principles will **presumably** lead to good health, a youthful appearance, and longevity.

Americans' preoccupation with fitness is apparent everywhere. How-
20 ever, fitness for its own sake is not the only motivation. Vanity is another incentive; looking attractive and *feeling "up"* builds self-confidence. Moreover, **frequenting** spas and health clubs provides a means for meeting people. It is a way of spontaneously making new acquaintances and friends.

The intense interest in the condition and appearance of the body has
25 generated a steady flow of highly marketable **innovations.** In fact, consumers spend billions of dollars annually on activities and products in their **quest** for fitness. Health clubs and fitness spas have sprouted throughout the nation, and many people sign up for lifetime memberships. Others, who prefer convenience and privacy, set up nautilus equipment in their own homes. The

30 fashion industry has designed eye-catching, functional apparel specifically for athletic activities. Many people shop in health food stores for organically grown goods and dietary supplements to add extra vitamins to their diets.

The concern for health has spread to other areas, too. Now, airlines offer a variety of meal choices to their passengers in addition to the regular menu:
35 vegetarian, low-calorie, salt-free. In restaurants as well as on planes, no-smoking areas are set aside for people who are concerned with safeguarding their health.

For many years, it has been the practice of giant corporations to maintain a gym or health club for the exclusive use of their executives. By working
40 out at the gym, or playing tennis, the top people in management could release some of the tensions generated at work. Membership in these corporate facilities was, and still is, a **status symbol.** Currently, however, a new attitude is **emerging.** All employees are burdened with tensions and pressures and could benefit from this type of recreation. As a matter of fact, studies have
45 indicated that improvement in physical and mental fitness contributes substantially to employee productivity. Fewer sick-day absences is also a financial gain for the company. It therefore makes good sense for major corporations to offer health club memberships to *all* their employees. This concept is revolutionary, but it is one that is being considered seriously. General Motors,
50 one of America's largest manufacturers of automobiles, has recently provided "wellness" benefits for all their employees. This policy is a **radical** change from illness and hospitalization **coverage.** It is a **milestone** that will surely lead to more meaningful and diversified benefits in the future.

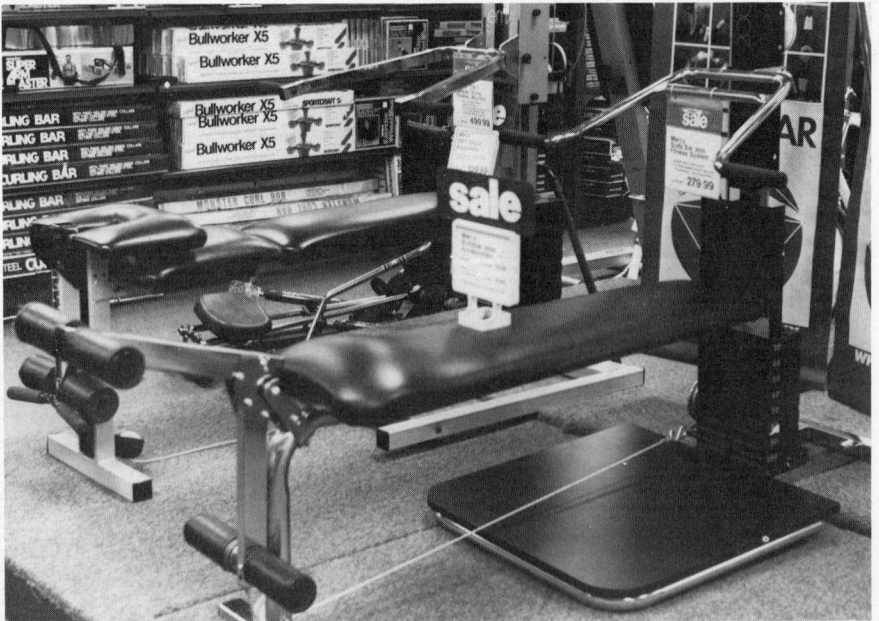

Some industrial giants maintain their own **elaborate** recreational facili-
55 ties that may include basketball and tennis courts, exercise rooms, steam
rooms and sauna baths, swimming pools, and a jogging track. Some large
companies have professionals conduct classes aimed at improving diet, quitting smoking, and dealing with stress. Smaller firms without their own facilities offer some of these benefits by paying for membership in commercial
60 clubs.

There is no doubt about it: When people are physically fit, they are at
their best. It makes sense to maintain optimum health in order to live life to
the fullest.

A. True/False Statements

After reading the passage for the first time, read the following statements and
check whether they are True (T) or False (F).

_____ T _____ F   1. Information on fitness programs and diets is available
only from doctors.

_____ T _____ F   2. People are interested in being fit only for the sake of
their appearance.

_____ T _____ F   3. Some people join spas in order to meet people.

_____ T _____ F   4. A spa is the only place to exercise.

_____ T _____ F   5. Many businesses have developed merchandise and services to meet the fitness demand.

_____ T _____ F   6. Corporate health clubs used to be for executives only.

_____ T _____ F   7. Many companies have begun to see the benefits of helping keep their employees healthy.

B. Comprehension Questions

1. The main idea of the article is:
   a. Americans have become very concerned with health and fitness, and
   this concern has influenced many aspects of American life.
   b. Americans' concern with their health has led to higher vitamin sales.
   c. Because Americans are interested in fitness, they have begun to exercise regularly and eat healthier foods.
   d. In order to work out regularly, many Americans keep equipment in
   their homes.
2. What are the qualities of a physically fit person?
3. How do people get information on exercise programs and nutrition?

4. What varied reasons do people have for becoming and keeping fit?
5. How has the concern for health spread to other areas?
6. What have many large corporations begun to consider seriously?
7. Why have these corporations begun to consider changing their policies?

C. Vocabulary in Context Exercise: Part I

A. Read the sentences below carefully, and try to understand the meaning of the boldface words.
   1. Monica wanted to lose fifteen pounds, so she went on a careful diet. Because she **adhered to** the diet faithfully, she was able to lose fifteen pounds in a month.
   2. Fae wanted to go to college very much. When she learned that she had been accepted to the college of her choice and that she had been given a scholarship, she was **ecstatic!** She had never been so happy in her entire life.
   3. Studying in a cooking school **encompasses** not only the art of cooking but also food buying, food serving, and restaurant management.
   4. Ever since I became interested in history, I have begun **frequenting** old bookstores, looking for interesting old history books.
   5. Advertising has **pervaded** our lives. It is on television, on the radio, in newspapers and magazines, and even on billboards on highways. We even receive advertisements in the mail!
   6. I spoke to Audrey and she said she would arrive at 1:00 P.M. It is now 1:15 P.M. and someone is ringing my door bell. **Presumably,** Audrey is at the door.
   7. After the car accident, the policeman asked the first driver what had happened, and the man told him. Then, the policeman asked the second driver what had happened. Finally, the policeman asked a witness what had happened. In the end, he had three different **versions** of the accident.
   8. Susan is not lazy. Everything she does, she does with **vigor.** She is enthusiastic and puts considerable effort into everything.
B. Match the following words with the definitions and synonyms listed below.

adhere to	encompass	pervade	version
ecstatic	frequent (v.)	presumably	vigor

1. _____ : delighted; overjoyed

2. _____ : include

3. _____ : spread throughout

4. _____ : energy

5. _____ : an account or description from a particular point of view

6. _____ : follow; hold; maintain

7. _____ : probably; supposedly

8. _____ : visit often

C. Vocabulary in Context Exercise: Part II

A. Read the sentences below carefully, and try to understand the meaning of the boldface words.
   1. In most states in the United States, in order to drive a car, you must have accident **coverage.** In fact, if your car is not insured, you cannot legally drive it.
   2. Richard and Terri have a very **elaborate** kitchen in their house. In addition to a regular oven, they have a microwave oven and fourteen different modern appliances.
   3. John has always been a very quiet man. As a result, it was several years before his considerable abilities **emerged** and he became an important executive in his company.
   4. When the automobile was first seen on American roads, it was considered a dirty, noisy, useless **innovation.** People used to laugh at motorists as they drove by.
   5. When the process of immunization was developed, it was a **milestone** in the elimination of diseases all over the world. Never before did people have such control over such serious illnesses as polio and smallpox.
   6. The campers went all over the mountain in their **quest** for a source of water. Once they found a small spring, they marked it carefully on their maps.
   7. Joan had always been a very calm, quiet, polite person. One day she became angry and began shouting. Everyone was surprised at the **radical** change in her behavior.
   8. To many Americans, having a house in the suburbs and driving a large, powerful car are **status symbols.** Without these two things, they feel like ordinary people.
B. Match the following words with the definitions and synonyms listed below.

coverage   emerge   milestone   radical
elaborate   innovation   quest   status symbol

1. _____ : novelty; something new

2. _____ : search

3. _____ : a sign of high rank or prestige

4. _____ : become known; arise

5. _____ : extreme; drastic

6. _____ : insurance

7. _____ : a significant point in any development

8. _____ : complex; sophisticated

D. Detailed Comprehension Exercise

Answer the following questions. Refer back to the passage wherever necessary.

1. " . . . Ponce de Leon stirred up a great deal of hope when he proclaimed that he had discovered the Fountain of Youth. . . . " (lines 1–2)

   What does **stirred up** mean? _____

2. "Being young has universal appeal. Even today, . . . people are searching for the qualities that youth encompasses. . . . " (lines 3–5)

   What is the purpose of *even* in this context? _____

3. "Via the media, we are constantly bombarded with suggestions to be slim, do exercise, and feel fit." (lines (7–9)

   What does **bombarded** mean? _____

4. "Newspapers and magazines regularly feature columns that present the latest nutritional discoveries and exercise equipment. In fact, it is almost impossible to pick up a general interest magazine and not find the perfect diet and easy exercise programs." (lines 10–13)

   How does *in fact* connect what follows it to what precedes it? _____

   _____

5. "Countless books and tapes on fitness are available in bookstores and libraries." (lines 14–15)

   What does **countless** mean in this context? _____

6. " . . . fitness for its own sake is not the only motivation." (line 20)

   What does **for its own sake** mean? _____

7. "Vanity is another incentive; looking attractive and **feeling 'up'** builds self-confidence." (lines 20–21)

   a. How does the semicolon connect the two thoughts in this sentence?

   _____

   b. What does **feeling "up"** mean? _____

8. "It is a way of spontaneously making new acquaintances and friends." (line 23)
What is the difference between an acquaintance and a friend?

_____

9. "Health clubs and fitness spas have sprouted throughout the nation. . . . " (line 27)

What does **sprouted** mean? _____

10. "The fashion industry has designed eye-catching, functional apparel. . . . " (lines 29 – 30)
Look at the word **eye-catching**. What does it mean?

_____

11. "In restaurants as well as on planes, no-smoking areas are set aside for people who are concerned with safeguarding their health." (lines 35 – 37)

a. What does **set aside** mean? _____

b. What does **safeguard** mean? _____

c. How do you know? _____

12. For many years, it has been the practice of giant corporations to maintain a gym or health club for the exclusive use of their executives." (lines 38 – 39)

a. What does **practice** mean in this context? _____

b. What does **exclusive** mean? _____

13. "All employees . . . could benefit from this type of recreation. As a matter of fact, studies have indicated that improvement in physical and mental fitness contributes substantially to employee productivity." (lines 43 – 46)
How does *as a matter of fact* relate what follows it to what precedes it?

_____

14. "Fewer sick-day absences is also a financial gain for the company. It therefore makes good sense for major corporations to offer health club memberships to *all* their employees." (lines 46 – 48)
a. *Therefore* introduces a conclusion. What is the conclusion to be drawn

here? _____

b. Why is *all* emphasized? _____

15. " . . . When people are physically fit, they are at their best." (lines 61 – 62)

What does **at their best** mean? _____

16. "It makes sense to maintain optimum health in order to live life to the fullest." (lines 62 – 63)

What does this statement mean? _____

E. Vocabulary in Context Quiz

Complete each blank space with a synonym of the word(s) in parentheses. You may need to use more than one word.

We Americans are very much involved in the (1)_____
(search)
for fitness. Fitness (2) _____ the qualities of good health,
(includes)
mental alertness, physical attractiveness, and (3) _____. The
(energy)
pursuit of this goal (4) _____ our daily lives in many ways.
(has spread throughout)
The media (5) _____ us with the virtues of being slim, doing
(persistently attack)
exercise, and feeling fit. Television programs, magazines, and newspapers always feature much information on fitness. Doctors also advocate being slender

and (6) _____ time to exercise regularly. They claim that if
(allowing)
we (7) _____ this advice, we will enjoy good health, longev-
(follow)
ity, and a youthful appearance. For most of us, the young look is a source of self-confidence.

The high interest in self-improvement has brought on many marketable

(8)_____. High fashion, eye-catching clothing designed
(novelties)
(9) _____ for exercise and sports has become big business.
(solely)
Many health spas have opened throughout the nation; people

(10) _____ these spas not only for workouts but also for
(often visit)
friendship. In addition, health food stores prosper because many of us believe

natural foods help (11) _____ their health. Low-calorie, die-
(protect)
tetic foods help people reduce; they feel (12) _____ when
(delighted)
they reach their desired weight.

It has been the (13) _____ of large corporations to main-
(habit)
tain health clubs for their executive officers. Being permitted to use these

facilities was a (14) _____ . A new attitude about this execu-
(sign of prestige)

tive benefit is (15) _____ : workouts at health clubs could im-
(arising)

prove the condition of all employees. This (16) _____ new
(extremely)

idea is being proposed by union officials. (17) _____ , the rec-
(Supposedly)

reation that relieves tension for high executives will do the same for tension

of lower-status employees. A recent contract with General Motors in-

cluded some wellness benefits. Until now, only illness and hospitalization

(18) _____ was detailed in union contracts. This consideration
(insurance)

of wellness is a (19) _____ in employee benefits. Future con-
(significant point)

tracts will surely offer new (20) _____ of wellness benefits.
(descriptions)

Meanwhile, people are making a great effort on their own to be fit and

look fit.

F. Topics for Discussion and Composition

1. What is the difference between good health and youthfulness? Is youthfulness a realistic goal? Why? Why not?
2. How far should restrictions go in protecting the health of nonsmokers? For
   example, should all businesses and public places provide smoking and
   nonsmoking areas? Should they prohibit smoking altogether?
3. Organically grown food is food that has been produced without any chemicals or insecticides. How beneficial is this type of food in comparison to
   foods grown in the conventional way?
4. What does *live life to the fullest* mean to you?

Is Progress Always Improvement?

Introductory Questions

1. Someone once said, "We are what we eat." What do you think this statement means?
2. How can we eat three meals a day, never be hungry, and still be undernourished?
3. Are all foods in our supermarkets nutritious? Why? Why not?
4. How can we purchase foods when they are "out of season"?

Is Progress Always Improvement?

Supermarkets really are super markets! Almost every imaginable food is displayed along the aisles: in-season food, out-of-season food, fresh food, frozen food, prepared food, **concentrated** food, dietetic food, domestic food, imported food, and imitation food. Selections are unlimited, labels are eye-
5 catching, and supplies are bountiful. It is not at all difficult to put together a mouth-watering feast, either by cooking **from scratch** or by using labor-saving **convenience foods.** The challenge is to produce a nutritious, well-balanced meal. That is not an easy task.

The variety and terminology of foods can be perplexing and misleading
10 to the uninformed shopper. Shopping for such staples as cheese and fruit juice is not as simple a process as it used to be. New terms have been created for new types of food. Years ago, cheese was correctly **assumed** to be real, pure cheese. Today we have not only cheese but also processed cheese, cheese food, cheese-flavored food, and imitation cheese. Similarly, fruit juice is just
15 that, whereas fruit drink contains less than 20 percent actual juice. Imitation fruit drink contains no juice at all.

If the **nomenclature** on the front of the label is bewildering, the details on the back of the label furnish clear information about the contents of the package. One important source of information for the shopper, or consumer,
20 is the list of ingredients that is required by law on all food labels. By reading the ingredients, the consumer will know the exact amount of water, the kinds of chemicals, the nutritional value of the food, the calorie count, and the sodium, or salt, content. The ingredients are listed in descending order of quantity. For example, a can of vegetable soup will list water first, since it is
25 mostly water, then list carrots, potatoes, celery, and so on. There are more carrots than potatoes, and more potatoes than celery. The label also indicates the vitamin and mineral content and lists the percentage of the recommended daily allowance (RDA) for each. For the consumer who is concerned with nutrition and good health, this information is essential. Some food products

30 that are widely used by the public contain no element of **sound** nutrition. In
fact, certain foods are harmful in some ways in spite of their appealing taste
and appearance. These foods are called junk foods. Soda and candy are prime
examples of a food in this category. Millions of people enjoy soda for various
reasons **irrespective of** the fact that its nutritional benefit is nil and that it
35 causes tooth decay. This listing of ingredients and nutritional values is a wise
place to start, but the search for information does not end there.

Food chemists have developed chemicals to increase the **longevity** of
food products. This is a significant factor in food production for several reasons. First of all, it makes it possible for food to be transported to distant
40 places without deteriorating, or spoiling. Secondly, it is economically advan-
tageous to manufacturers and storekeepers for foods to have a long shelf life.
Finally, consumers can **store** foods at home for extended periods of time.
Although chemicals effectively preserve food, there is considerable controversy regarding their potential harm. Many manufacturers claim that these
45 additives are innocuous, while consumer groups insist that they are detrimental to one's health. In the face of this controversy, the wisest decision for
shoppers to make is to purchase foods with a minimum of chemicals.

Dates are an additional **pertinent** feature on labels of **perishable** foods.
Basically, these fall into two categories: *expiration date* and *sell-by* date. The
50 former indicates either that the product is not usable after that date, or that
it loses its full nutritional value. The *sell-by* date indicates the day the product
must be removed from the store shelves. It does not mean that the product
is **inedible.** For example, a container of milk marked May 1 should still be
drinkable on May 3 if it has been properly stored, but it cannot be sold after
55 May 1 (it must be *sold by* May 1).

Advanced technology has enabled manufacturers to produce many foods
in convenient forms. A case in point is coffee. In the supermarket, coffee is

**PERCENTAGE OF U.S. RECOMMENDED
DAILY ALLOWANCES (U.S. RDA)**

PROTEIN	6	15
VITAMIN A	25	30
VITAMIN C	25	25
THIAMIN	25	30
RIBOFLAVIN	25	35
NIACIN	25	25
CALCIUM	4	20
IRON	25	25
VITAMIN D	10	25
VITAMIN B₆	25	30
VITAMIN B₁₂	25	35
PHOSPHORUS	10	20
MAGNESIUM	10	15
ZINC	6	8
COPPER	6	6

INGREDIENTS: WHOLE OAT FLOUR, WHEAT STARCH, SALT,
SUGAR, CALCIUM CARBONATE, TRISODIUM PHOSPHATE,
SODIUM ASCORBATE (VITAMIN C), NIACIN (A B VITAMIN),
IRON (A MINERAL NUTRIENT), VITAMIN A PALMITATE,
PYRIDOXINE HYDROCHLORIDE (VITAMIN B₆), RIBOFLAVIN

actually 100 percent coffee. It is also available decaffeinated. Moreover, it can be bought not only in various grinds ready to be **brewed** but also in instant
60 and freeze-dried form. In all cases, the product is pure coffee; however, the flavor is affected by each process.

For the intelligent shopper, **scrutinizing** labels carefully is a worth-while **investment** of time for a continuing nutritional **payoff**. After deter-mining which product of a particular group is most desirable, the consumer
65 can make repeat purchases automatically. Even though many shoppers ignore the given information, the facts are accessible to those who wish to be pru-dent consumers.

A. True/False Statements

After reading the passage for the first time, read the following statements and indicate whether they are True (T) or False (F).

_____ T _____ F   1. Putting together a nutritious, well-balanced meal is easy.

_____ T _____ F   2. There is no difference between fruit juice and fruit drink.

_____ T _____ F   3. Food is as pure and natural as it was many years ago.

_____ T _____ F   4. The terms *expiration date* and *sell-by date* do not have the same meaning.

_____ T _____ F   5. Chemists disagree whether or not chemicals in foods are harmless.

_____ T _____ F   6. It is important for the intelligent food shopper to read food labels carefully.

B. Comprehension Questions

1. The main idea of the article is:
   a. Labels give important nutritional information as well as the list of in-gredients.
   b. Many changes have taken place in types of food available in supermar-kets.
   c. Colorful pictures on labels, while attractive, do not reflect the quality of the product.
   d. Food shopping is a complex process, so shoppers should be well in-formed.
2. Ingredients are listed in descending order on labels. What does this mean?
3. What does "shelf life" mean?
4. What is the difference between an expiration date and a sell-by date?

5. Why are manufacturers and storekeepers happy about the changes in food production?
6. Why does a wise consumer read labels all the time?

C. Vocabulary in Context Exercise: Part I

A. Read the sentences below carefully, and try to understand the meaning of the boldface words.
1. John said that he would drive to our house and pick us up at 6:30. It is now 6:29 and I hear a car outside. I **assume** it is John in the car.
2. Many people drink instant coffee, but I prefer to **brew** it in a regular coffee pot. It may take more time, but the flavor is much better.
3. When you buy frozen orange juice, it is always **concentrated.** To make it taste like fresh orange juice, you need to add water. Then it will have a natural flavor.
4. Since television has become so popular, many food companies have begun to produce TV dinners. These are prepared meals on a tray. They are frozen. All you need to do is to heat them in an oven and eat them. These **convenience foods** have become very popular, too.
5. Victoria likes to buy a box of cake mix and simply add eggs and water in order to bake a cake. Harriet, on the other hand, prefers to bake cakes **from scratch.** She measures out the flour, salt, and other ingredients carefully and even melts the chocolate herself if it is a chocolate cake.
6. Victoria and Harriet decided to test which type of cake was better, so they each prepared a cake: one from a mix, the other from scratch. Harriet's cake was delicious, but Victoria's cake was **inedible** and they had to throw it out.
7. Ellie wanted to start her own business, but she needed money. Ann made an **investment** of $10,000, and Ellie's business was successful. She was able to pay back the $10,000 she had borrowed, plus an additional $2,000 in interest. Ann had obviously made a wise **investment!**
8. Debbie did not want to go bicycling in the country. She protested loudly against the idea. **Irrespective of** her arguments, Mark rented two bicycles and insisted that Debbie go bicycling with him.
9. There is a group of people in Georgia in the Caucasus Mountains who are well known for their **longevity;** many of them live to the age of 100 years or more.
B. Match the following words with the definitions and synonyms listed below.

assume   concentrated   from scratch   investment   longevity
brew   convenience food   inedible   irrespective of

1. _____ : from the basic ingredients

2. _____ : prepare a beverage such as tea, chocolate, and so on

3. _____ : without regard to; independent of

4. _____ : suppose; take for granted

5. _____ : food bought for immediate use

6. _____ : length of life

7. _____ : strong; undiluted; intense

8. _____ : uneatable; not fit for food

9. _____ : commitment of something to an interest or project

C. Vocabulary in Context Exercise: Part II

A. Read the sentences below carefully, and try to understand the meaning of the boldface words.

1. Many people who are not familiar with computers do not understand the **nomenclature.** They do not understand conversations between computer scientists when they talk about *turnaround time* or say that the computer was *down* for two days.

2. Natalie worked hard for many years for the same company without being noticed by her supervisors. Her **payoff** finally came, however, when her supervisor suddenly quit and she was asked to take the job. She performed so well that she was promoted to manager.

3. Like milk, cream is highly **perishable.** Therefore, you should buy it when you plan to use it. If you keep it for more than three days, you will have to throw it away and buy a fresh container.

4. Nancy was found murdered and the police arrested her husband, Tom. Although he claimed he was innocent, the lawyers thought it was very **pertinent** that he and Nancy had had a terrible fight the night before the murder and that Tom was the last person to see her alive.

5. Before buying any clothes in a store, **scrutinize** them for loose threads, poorly sewn seams, and loose or missing buttons.

6. Joseph is always able to make **sound** decisions because he takes the time to collect all important information first, and then to study the information carefully. He rarely makes wrong decisions as a result.

7. The people who live in areas where the winter weather is severe must plan carefully and **store** food in case they are forced to stay in their homes because of heavy snowfall and freezing cold. They usually begin to **store** dry and canned food in their basements, and **store** vegetables at the end of the summer in their kitchens.

B. Match the following words with the definitions and synonyms listed below.

nomenclature   perishable   scrutinize   store
payoff   pertinent   sound

1. _____ : relevant; has a connection or relation with something

2. _____ : collect as a reserve supply; lay away

3. _____ : reward; profit

4. _____ : correct; reliable

5. _____ : a system of names or designations; terminology

6. _____ : examine closely; inspect

7. _____ : not durable; cannot be conserved indefinitely

D. Detailed Comprehension Exercise

Answer the following questions. Refer back to the passage wherever necessary.

1. "Supermarkets really are super markets!" (line 1) This line represents a play on words in the use of *super* and *market*.

   a. What is a **supermarket?** _____

b. Why are supermarkets super? _____

2. "Almost every imaginable food is displayed along the aisles: in-season
    food, out-of-season food. . . . " (lines 1–2)

    a. What is food that is in season? _____

    b. What is food that is out of season? _____

3. " . . . labels are eye-catching. . . . " (lines 4–5)

    Analyze the word **eye-catching.** What does it mean? _____

4. "It is not at all difficult to put together a mouth-watering feast."
    (lines 5–6)

    Analyze the word **mouth-watering.** What does it mean? _____

5. What do **labor-saving** foods do? (See line 6.) _____

6. "The variety and terminology of foods can be perplexing and misleading
    to the uninformed shopper." (lines 9–10)
    Read the rest of paragraph 2. If you didn't know, for example, the differ-

    ence between fruit drink and fruit juice, how would you be misled? ____

    _____

7. "Today we have not only cheese but also processed cheese, cheese food,
    cheese-flavored food, and imitation cheese." (lines 13–14)
    How do the words *not only* and *but also* connect the terms *cheese, cheese*

    food, cheese-flavored food, and *imitation cheese?* _____

    _____

8. ". . . fruit juice is just that, whereas fruit drink contains less than 20
    percent actual juice." (lines 14–15)

    a. What does **just that** mean? _____

    b. What does **whereas** mean? _____

9. "If the nomenclature on the front of the label is bewildering, the details
    on the back of the label furnish clear information about the contents of
    the package." (lines 17–19)
    What does **if** mean in this context? In other words, how does it relate the
    information in the first part of the sentence with the information in the

    second part of the sentence? _____

10. ". . . the list of ingredients that is required by law on all food labels."
    (line 20)

    a. What is meant by this phrase? _____

    b. What are **ingredients?** _____

11. "The ingredients are listed in descending order of quantity. For example,

a can of vegetable soup will list water first, since it is mostly water, then list carrots, potatoes, celery, and so on." (lines 23–25)

a. What does **descending order** mean? _____

b. How do you know? _____

12. "The label also indicates the vitamin and mineral content and lists the percentage of the recommended daily allowance (RDA) for each." (lines 26–28)

a. What do the letters *RDA* stand for? _____

b. Why is this information useful? _____

13. "Some food products that are widely used by the public contain no element of sound nutrition. In fact, certain foods are harmful in some ways in spite of their appealing taste and appearance." (lines 29–32)

How does *in fact* relate what precedes it to what follows it? _____

_____

14. "Millions of people enjoy soda for various reasons irrespective of the fact that its nutritional benefit is nil and that it causes tooth decay." (lines 33–35)

a. What does **nil** mean? _____

b. How do you know? _____

15. Reread paragraph 4.

a. What does **shelf life** mean? _____

b. How do you know? _____

16. "Many manufacturers claim that these additives are innocuous, while consumer groups insist that they are detrimental to one's health." (lines 44–46)

a. How does *while* connect what precedes it with what follows it? _____

_____

b. What does **innocuous** mean? _____

17. "Advanced technology has enabled manufacturers to produce many foods in convenient forms. A case in point is coffee." (lines 56–57)

What does **a case in point** mean? _____

18. "Even though many shoppers ignore the given information, the facts are accessible to those who wish to be prudent consumers." (lines 65–67)

a. What does **even though** mean? _____

b. What does **accessible** mean? _____

c. How do you know? _____

d. What does *the given information* refer to? _____

_____

E. Vocabulary in Context Quiz

Complete each blank space with a synonym of the word(s) in parentheses. You may need to use more than one word.

    Shopping in supermarkets is an adventure in food. There are endless, tempting varieties. The aisles are full of choices for the cook who wants to start (1)_____ , and also choices for the cook who wants to
(from basic ingredients)
use (2) _____ . Food technology has advanced to the
(foods bought for immediate use)
point of satisfying choices for everyone. It is quite easy to prepare a(n)

(3) _____ ,   tasty   meal.   However,   we   cannot
(appetizing)
(4) _____ that everything we buy is nutritious.
(take for granted)
    Labels are somewhat strange. The (5)_____ on labels
(terminology)
is sometimes misleading; think of cheese-flavored food. On the other hand, clear, factual information can also be found on labels. All manufacturers are required by law to have a list of the (6) _____ on their food
(contents)
labels. Labels also indicate the vitamin and mineral content. This is essential for the shopper who is concerned with (7) _____ nutrition.
(correct)
    Another aspect of many foods is their chemical content. Chemicals to prolong (8) _____ are widely used. This practice enables food
(length of life)
to be delivered to distant places without (9) _____ ; it can
(spoiling)
have a long shelf life in stores. Consumers can (10) _____
(lay away)
many products for a long time at home. There is continuing controversy about the   chemicals   used   in   foods.   Manufacturers   claim   that   they   are

(11) _____, while consumer groups insist that they are dan-
        (harmless)

gerous.

(12) _____   foods   have   additional
        (nondurable)

(13) _____ information on labels. One is an *expiration date* or
        (relevant)

a *sell-by date*. The former indicates that the product should not be used after

that date, whereas the *sell-by* date tells the storekeeper to remove the prod-

uct from the shelf even though it might still be (14) _____ ;
                                                        (fit to be eaten)

a(n) (15) _____ is cheese.
              (example)

It is apparent that a(n) (16) _____ of time in
                                    (commitment)

(17) _____ labels can result in a valuable nutritional
        (closely examining)

(18) _____. (19) _____ all the junk food that
        (reward)   (In spite of)

is (20) _____ in food stores today, choices can be made by
            (available)

prudent shoppers.

F. Topics for Discussion and Composition

1. How can we be better informed and more selective consumers?
2. What do the following terms mean? (a) processed cheese; (b) cheese food; (c) cheese-flavored; (d) imitation cheese. What is the implication behind these terms?
3. What is the difference between ground coffee, instant coffee, and freeze-dried coffee?
4. The author implies, but does not directly state, that improvement is not always positive. What changes are really improvements, and what changes are negative changes?
5. Compare a meal you have made from scratch with a convenience food meal with regard to (a) the time involved, (b) the cost, and (c) the nutritional value.

12

Pet Therapy

Introductory Questions

1. How can pets be a substitute for human companionship in periods of loneliness?
2. What desirable qualities does a pet such as a dog or cat have that are difficult to find in friends?
3. How can a pet enrich a person's life in a way that a person cannot?
4. Do you know anyone who grew to think of a pet as a human member of the family? Why do you think they felt this way?
5. How can pets improve the quality of their owners' lives?

Pet Therapy

People who are troubled by ailments visit doctors or therapists in search of good health. Doctors have traditionally prescribed pills, liquid medications, dietary modifications, rest, exercise. "Take two pills three times a day" is a very familiar order to most of us. Currently, however, doctors are beginning
5 to **count on** a new therapeutic device with which to treat certain conditions. This therapy is radically different; it has no resemblance to medication. This "medicine" is alive and emotionally responsive. This new kind of doctor's prescription is a pet. Pet therapy is a new area being explored in the fields of physical and mental health, and the potential benefits are very **promising.**
10 Recent data show a strong link between having a pet and good health and longevity. Pets enhance life in different ways. The most popular pets in the United States are cats and dogs; birds, fish, turtles, hamsters, and gerbils are also favorites, especially among young children. While most pets provide benefits, dogs will be the pet referred to in this passage.
15 There is an old saying, "Dog is man's best friend." People have long enjoyed the **unqualified** affection that dogs give. Dog owners have **invariably** described their pets in terms of affection, companionship, trust, loyalty, fun, obedience, protection, and safety. These admirable qualities are difficult to find in our friends, yet we can find an **assortment** of good qualities in a pet!
20 Dog is certainly a person's best friend, and current research has given even deeper meaning to this saying.
Remarkable data have emerged from research on pets and people with physical and mental disorders. In many cases, pets bring about health gains where other therapies and medications were ineffective. In one study, two
25 groups of patients, one having pets, the other not, were compared. The former showed dramatic **strides** in health and positive attitudes. To illustrate,

heart attack patients owning pets recovered more quickly than those without pets. Furthermore, blood pressure in the former group dropped more readily within the normal range. In fact, doctors have found that pet owners in gen-
30 eral enjoy better health and longevity and have higher **resistance** to disease than those who don't own pets.

Mental patients **thrive** in a unique relationship with pets. These patients gradually build friendship and trust, and often unburden themselves of emotions that they had never expressed before. Pets somehow affect patients in a
35 manner that diminishes strongly **embedded** fears. Pets are the keys that unlock doors to suppressed emotions.

In everyday life, too, having a pet is beneficial to people of all ages. The love that **emanates from** a dog is unique. A dog is totally nonjudgmental, and its loyalty is unquestioning and constant. When children are scolded, or re-
40 primanded, they can always depend on their four-legged friends to lend a sympathetic, uncritical ear. After a tongue-lashing from parents, children are substantially comforted by an affectionate tongue licking from their dogs. This gesture transmits a big dose of love, which helps heal hurt feelings. When children are in a quiet mood, not only is the act of petting, or stroking, a dog
45 comforting, but it also creates a bond of intimacy. When youngsters are in high spirits and **rambunctious,** dogs are cooperative playmates. They run with determination to retrieve a ball or stick; they can be taught to do assorted tricks; they "play-fight" with vigor. They are lots of fun.

Dogs are also a **stabilizing** influence for adolescents, who often experi-
50 ence **turbulent** emotions. Dogs are very sensitive and friendly companions. The comfort they provide diminishes feelings of **alienation** from **peers** and parents. Holding or petting a dog is a peaceful break from the complexities of life. In addition, when children have to take care of their pets, this duty helps build a sense of responsibility that will serve them well for the rest of their
55 lives.

Dogs provide companionship for adults, too. They are a reliable source of affection and loyalty. Nothing can compare to the jubilant welcome that dogs express when family members return home after being out. While dogs make minimal demands, they provide limitless rewards. In addition to the
60 emotional benefits, having to walk dogs is good exercise for the walkers. Moreover, walking a dog provides an opportunity for spontaneous socializing. People strike up conversations more easily when dogs are in the picture. Dogs are a natural topic of conversation for shy people. They enjoy boasting about their pets.

65 Dogs are incomparable companions for the elderly living in their own homes. They become loving friends and add structure and meaning to life. When people pet and talk to dogs, their level of stress is reduced. The responsibility of taking care of their dogs gives purpose and structure to their lives. Feeling needed is positive reinforcement of self-worth. Pets also relieve
70 feelings of loneliness and isolation. "Somebody" is always there, loving and loyal. The elderly also feel safer because of their pets. Barking dogs have **deterred** many intruders **from** their criminal plans or successfully attacked

those who did enter the home. The media frequently report instances in which dogs barked frantically to alert their owners to a spreading fire.

75   Recently the American Society for the Prevention of Cruelty to Animals (A.S.P.C.A.) has begun a program to bring dogs to residences for the aged twice a week. This direct contact with animals has been therapeutic for the residents. They look forward to holding, hugging, and petting the dogs; it is an uplifting break in their otherwise predictable, **uninspired** routines. There
80 is an exchange of love, warmth, and intimacy between humans and animals. All too often the elderly receive no such attention from people, so these visits provide a priceless mental lift. In fact, this pet therapy is "medicine that the doctor ordered"—"medicine" that is much more effective than drugs.

      Day in and day out, pets provide companionship and pleasurable activ-
85 ity; are living, responsive beings to care for; are dependable and constantly "there"; stimulate play, laughter, and exercise; provide **solace** through the sense of touch; offer unqualified love; generate a feeling of safety.

      Although dogs were chosen as the pet reference in this passage, all pets offer invaluable benefits. With health professionals opening up broader hori-
90 zons in health care through pet therapy, pet ownership is a medical option that is increasingly being considered.

A. True/False Statements

After reading the passage for the first time, read the following statements and check whether they are True (T) or False (F).

_____ T _____ F   1. Doctors are starting to use pets as a kind of therapy.

_____ T _____ F   2. People who have pets are always healthy.

_____ T _____ F   3. Blood pressure can be affected by a pet.

_____ T _____ F   4. Mental patients do not benefit from having a pet.

_____ T _____ F   5. Dogs help prevent crime.

_____ T _____ F   6. Only children and the elderly benefit from having pets.

B. Comprehension Questions

1. The main idea of the article is:
    a. Research is rapidly growing, showing the value of pets as therapeutic aids.
    b. People have begun to look at pets and pet owners in a new way.
    c. Pets help shy people talk because they are a natural topic of conversation.
    d. It has been shown that people who own pets live longer than people who don't.
2. Why do people say that a "dog is man's best friend?"
3. In cases of such diseases as high blood pressure, how does having a pet benefit the patient?
4. How does having a pet benefit mental patients?
5. Why is a dog a good companion for a child?
6. Why is a dog a good companion for an adolescent?
7. Why is a dog a good companion for an elderly person?
8. How does the A.S.P.C.A. contribute to pet therapy?

C. Vocabulary in Context Exercise: Part I

A. Read the sentences below carefully, and try to understand the meaning of the boldface words.
    1. When José left Colombia and came to the United States, he was very unhappy. He didn't know anyone, and the language and customs were unfamiliar to him. It took him several months to overcome feelings of **alienation** and begin to feel as though he really belonged.
    2. I love shopping at the weekly produce market. There is always an **assortment** of fruit and vegetables to choose from. I can spend the entire day selecting the fruits and vegetables I like the best.
    3. You can always **count on** Walter; if he says he'll do something, he will surely do it. If he says he will remember something, he will be sure to remember it.
    4. Mr. and Mrs. McGrath put a fence around their yard to **deter** people **from** walking across the grass.

5. The water that **emanates from** this underground stream is pure enough to drink.

6. You will need tools to remove these nails from the wall because they are deeply **embedded** in the wood.

7. Whenever we plan to go on a picnic, it **invariably** rains. The last five times we made arrangements to go, it rained all day.

8. When Doctor Harrison presented his paper at a conference, his **peers** criticized him for his irrational conclusions. Because they had the same training and experience, Doctor Harrison respected their opinions.

9. Angela is a very **promising** teacher. She is well educated, imaginative, and sociable. She gets along well with her colleagues and the students. I'm sure she'll succeed in her new teaching position.

B. Match the following words with the definitions and synonyms listed below.

alienation   count on   emanate from   invariably   promising
assortment   deter   embedded   peer

1. _____ : enclosed

2. _____ : likely to give good results

3. _____ : depend on; rely on

4. _____ : variety; a number of different things

5. _____ : a feeling of withdrawal, unfriendliness, or in-
                       difference to people or places

6. _____ : discourage

7. _____ : consistently; without exception

8. _____ : come out from; spring from

9. _____ : a person of the same age, abilities, social stand-
                       ing, and so on

C. Vocabulary in Context Exercise: Part II

A. Read the sentences below carefully, and try to understand the meaning of the boldface words.

1. Timothy was a **rambunctious** child. Fortuantely, his mother was a very understanding woman, and she was able to control him when he became too wild.

2. Doctors stress the importance of a healthful diet in helping build **resistance** to illness. A nutritious diet will, in fact, help prevent getting certain illnesses, including the common cold.

3. When Mrs. Thorp's husband died, her grown children stayed with her

for several weeks. They were kind and understanding, and Mrs. Thorp derived considerable **solace** from their company and their sympathy.

4. The patient's blood pressure changed rapidly and became dangerously high. Her doctor prescribed a medication, which had a **stabilizing** effect on her blood pressure and kept it close to normal.

5. Since the beginning of the twentieth century, tremendous **strides** have been made in air travel. We have certainly improved airplanes, service, and airports since the early part of this century.

6. Most plants **thrive** in a warm, sunny environment when they are also given adequate water and plant food.

7. Martha always becomes very sick when she is in a boat during **turbulent** weather. The strong winds and high waves that rock the boat give her a serious case of motion sickness.

8. Anthony feels very **uninspired** by his routine office work. He does the same job every day and sees the same people. There is never anything new or interesting.

9. Tom and Judy's party was an **unqualified** success! The people were lively and interesting; the music was perfect for dancing; the food was plentiful and delicious; even the weather was perfect.

B. Match the following words with the definitions and synonyms listed below.

rambunctious	solace	strides	turbulent	unqualified
resistance	stabilizing	thrive	uninspired	

1. _____ : immunity; ability to withstand disease

2. _____ : advances; progress

3. _____ : uncontrollable; wild

4. _____ : unlimited; without any restrictions

5. _____ : comfort; consolation

6. _____ : unoriginal; lacking thought and development

7. _____ : steadying

8. _____ : stormy; violently disturbed

9. _____ : advance successfully; prosper

D. Detailed Comprehension Exercise

Answer the following questions. Refer back to the passage wherever necessary.

1. " 'Take two pills three times a day' is a very familiar order to most of us.

Currently, however, doctors are beginning to count on a new therapeutic device with which to treat certain conditions." (lines 3–5)

a. Why is *Take . . . day* in quotation marks? _____

_____

b. What is the function of *however* in this context? _____

_____

2. " . . . doctors are beginning to count on a new therapeutic device. . . . This therapy is radically different; it has no resemblance to medication." (lines 4–6)

a. What is the function of the semicolon in this sentence? _____

_____

b. What does **radically** mean? _____

3. "This 'medicine' is alive and emotionally responsive." (lines 6–7)

Why is *medicine* in quotation marks? _____

4. "Pet therapy is a new area being explored in the fields of physical and mental health. . . . " (lines 8–9)

What does **explored** mean in this context? _____

5. "Recent data show a strong link between having a pet and good health and longevity." (lines 10–11)

What does **link** mean? _____

6. "People have long enjoyed the unqualified affection that dogs give." (lines 15–16)

What does **long** mean here? _____

7. "In many cases [of physical and mental disorders], pets bring about health gains where other therapies and medications were ineffective." (lines 23–24)

What does **bring about** mean? _____

8. "In one study, two groups of patients, one having pets, the other not, were compared. The former showed dramatic strides in health and positive attitudes." (lines 24–26)

To whom does *the former* refer? _____

9. "To illustrate, heart attack patients owning pets recovered more quickly than those without pets. Furthermore, blood pressure in the former group dropped more readily within the normal range." (lines 26–29)

a. What does **to illustrate** mean here? _____
b. In the second line, what does *those without pets* refer to?

_____

c. What is the meaning of **furthermore?** _____

10. "In fact, doctors have found that pet owners in general enjoy better health and longevity. . . . " (lines 29–30)
What does **in general** mean? In other words, does this sentence describe

    every pet owner? _____

11. "Pets are the keys that unlock doors to suppressed emotions." (lines 35–36)
This sentence is a metaphor, or implied comparison. What are the keys,

    and what are the locked doors? _____

    _____

12. Using word analysis, look at the words **nonjudgmental** and **unquestioning** in lines 38–39.

    a. What does **nonjudgmental** mean? _____

    b. What does **unquestioning** mean? _____

13. "When children are scolded, or reprimanded, they can always depend on their four-legged friends to lend a sympathetic, uncritical ear." (lines 39–41)

    a. What is a synonym for **scolded?** _____

    b. How do you know? _____

    c. Who is the *four-legged friend?* _____

14. "After a tongue-lashing from parents, children are substantially comforted by an affectionate tongue licking from their dogs. This gesture transmits a big dose of love, which helps heal hurt feelings." (lines 41–43)
    a. What is the relationship between *tongue-lashing* and *tongue licking?*

    _____

    b. These two sentences present another metaphor, or implied comparison. In terms of pet therapy, answer the following:

       1. What is the wound, or injury? _____

       2. What is the **doctor's prescription?** _____

       3. What is the effect of this prescription? _____

15. "When children are in a quiet mood, not only is the act of petting, or stroking, a dog comforting, it also creates a bond of intimacy." (lines 43–45)

    a. What is a synonym of **petting?** _____

    b. How do you know? _____

    c. How does *not only* . . . *also* connect the two thoughts in the

       sentence? _____

16. "They run with determination to retrieve a ball or stick . . . they 'play-fight' with vigor." (lines 46 – 48)

a. What does **retrieve** mean? _____

b. Why is *play-fight* in quotation marks? _____

17. "Holding or petting a dog is a peaceful break from the complexities of life." (lines 52 – 53)
a. What is the difference between **holding** and **petting** a dog?

_____

b. What is a **peaceful break**? _____

18. "In addition, when children have the duty to take care of their pets, it helps build a sense of responsibility that will serve them well for the rest of their lives." (lines 53 – 55)

What does **it . . . will serve them well** mean? _____

19. "Nothing can compare to the jubilant welcome that dogs express when family members return home after being out." (lines 57 – 58)

What does **jubilant** mean? _____

20. "While dogs make minimal demands, they provide limitless rewards." (lines 58 – 59)
a. What idea does *while* introduce? In other words, what is the relation-

ship between the first half of this sentence and the second half ? _____

_____

b. What is the relationship between **minimal** and **limitless**?

_____

_____

21. "In addition to the emotional benefits, having to walk dogs is good exercise for the walkers. Moreover, walking a dog provides an opportunity for spontaneous socializing. People strike up conversations more easily when dogs are in the picture. Dogs are a natural topic of conversation for shy people." (lines 59 – 63)
a. Having a dog provides emotional benefits. What kind of benefits does

walking a dog provide? _____

b. How does *moreover* relate what precedes it to what follows it?

_____

c. How does the sentence *People strike up* . . . relate to the previous

sentence? _____

d. What does **strike up** mean? _____

e. What does **in the picture** mean? _____

f. How does the sentence *Dogs are a . . .* relate to the previous

sentence? _____

22. "Dogs are incomparable companions for the elderly. . . . " (line 65)

Using word analysis, define **incomparable.** _____

23. "Pets also relieve feelings of loneliness and isolation. 'Somebody' is always there, loving and loyal." (lines 69–71)

Why is *somebody* in quotation marks? _____

24. "There is an exchange of love, warmth, and intimacy between humans and animals. All too often the elderly receive no such attention from people. . . . " (lines 79–81)

What kind of attention does *such attention* refer to? _____

25. "In fact, this pet therapy is 'medicine that the doctor ordered'—'medicine' that is much more effective than drugs." (lines 82–83)

a. Why is *medicine that the doctor ordered* in quotation marks?

_____

b. Why is *medicine* in quotation marks? _____

26. "Day in and day out, pets provide companionship. . . . are dependable and constantly 'there' . . . " (lines 84–86)

a. **Day in and day out** means "every day." Why did the author choose

to use so many words to express this idea? _____

b. Why is *there* in quotation marks? _____

27. "With health professionals opening up broader horizons in health care through pet therapy, pet ownership is a medical option that is increasingly being considered." (lines 89–91)

a. What does **with** mean in this context? _____

b. What does **option** mean? _____

E. Vocabulary in Context Quiz

Complete each blank space with a synonym of the word(s) in parentheses. You may need to use more than one word.

In addition to traditional kinds of therapy in the field of medicine, pets

are now being used to promote good health. Pet therapy is a new method of

alleviating certain ailments, and it looks very (1)_____. There
(likely to give good results)

seems to be a unique (2) _____ between having a pet and
(connection)

enjoying good health. Companionship, loyalty, protection, fun, and, above all, (3) _____ affection are qualities in pets that people trea-
(unlimited)
sure. This (4) _____ of virtues is rare among human friends,
(variety)
yet a dog easily offers all of them.

Research shows that pet owners who have had heart attacks recover more readily than victims who don't have pets. In the field of mental health, doctors have made dramatic (5) _____, too. Patients who
(advances)
were withdrawn from the real world were able to express emotion to a pet. This very special relationship cuts through their intense (6) _____ in order to deal with reality. Doctors are
(immunity)
(7) _____ pets more and more as a therapeutic tool.
(relying on)
With children, too, dogs are a source of silent sympathy when parents (8) _____ them. For adolescents, dogs are often a(n)
(scold)
(9) _____ influence during (10) _____ peri-
(steadying)   (stormy)
ods. When youngsters are happy and (11) _____, dogs are
(uncontrollable)
eager playmates. They're always ready to (12) _____ a ball or
(bring back)
run or jump energetically. Not surprisingly, everyone, on coming home, likes the (13) _____ reception he or she receives—from the dog,
(very happy)
of course!

Dogs become intimate companions for the elderly who live alone. The elderly derive (14)_____ from dogs in many ways. Their close
(comfort)
relationship helps the aged (15) _____ physically and men-
(prosper)
tally. The understanding that their dogs need them for survival reinforces feelings of self-worth. Dogs also minimize feelings of (16) _____. Personal safety is another advantage because
(withdrawal)

barking dogs (17) _____ would-be intruders from entering
    (discourage)

their homes.

A program of bringing dogs to visit residents in old age homes has

proved therapeutic for these people. It is a welcome break in their

(18) _____, routine daily schedules. These visits are invalu-
    (unoriginal)

able; no medicine can do as much good.

It is obvious that pets almost (19) _____ improve the
                               (without exception)

quality of life of their owners. Pets are fast becoming a popular medical

(20) _____.
    (choice)

F. Topics for Discussion and Composition

1. Compare the kinds of relationships an owner would have with a pet such
   as a dog, a cat, or a bird.
2. How can an only child enjoy a pet?
3. What kind of pet would be most suitable for an elderly sick person? Why?
4. What sense of responsibility can children develop through having pets?

ANSWER KEY

Chapter I

Exercise A
1. F
2. T
3. F
4. T
5. T
6. T

Exercise B
1. a. too broad
   b. too narrow
   c. not mentioned
   d. main idea
2–6. Individual answers will vary.

Exercise C: Part I
B. 1. potential
   2. overcome
   3. profound
   4. reassurance
   5. anxious
   6. dwell on
   7. enthusiastically

Exercise C: Part II
B. 1. praise
   2. worthless
   3. goal
   4. spontaneous
   5. shame

Exercise D*
1. a. They are opposites.
   b. not smart; not intelligent
   c. too heavy; fat
2. a. It introduces an explanation of what came before it.
   b. being aware of or thinking about oneself too much
3. a. being anxious, self-conscious, and excessively concerned, and having worrisome thoughts
   b. They have a negative effect.
   c. negatively; in a bad way
4. a. It shows that this sentence is an explanation of the one before it.
   b. self-esteem
   c. by the phrase "or high self-esteem" set off by commas
5. It further explains the previous sentence.
6. Other people may be mistaken; they have no right to make decisions for you.
7. one of contrast
8. They show that paragraphs 2 and 3 are in opposition to each other.
9. The author implies that what is right for you is for you to decide, not for someone else to decide.

*Because the wording of individual answers will vary for Exercise D, all logical answers will be considered acceptable.

10. a. It is used like *although*.
    b. to do in excess
    c. harmful
    d. by the phrase "or harmful" set off by commas
11. a. get rid of
    b. decrease; lessen
12. a. The first part states a fact; the second part suggests a way of coping with it.
    b. because
13. a. jealousy
    b. When we envy someone else's accomplishment, which is unrealistic for us to achieve, we then become self-critical. This is self-destructive.
14. a. balance or proportion: one quality increases as the other decreases
    b. decrease
15. *Could* is underlined to emphasize the idea that your cooking, in reality, could actually improve.
16. a. It is an example of a disappointing experience with an unexpected happy ending.
    b. finding superior education where unsatisfactory quality education was expected

17. a. separate yourself from

Exercise E*
1. overweight
2. excessively
3. anxious
4. overdo
5. dwelling on
6. adversely
7. worthless
8. praise
9. potential
10. spontaneous
11. overcome
12. diminishing
13. instance
14. goal
15. excessively
16. detrimental
17. isolate
18. reduce
19. self-assurance
20. profound
21. envy
22. enthusiastically
23. since
24. Eliminate
25. self-esteem

CHAPTER 2

Exercise A
1. F
2. F
3. T
4. F
5. T

Exercise B
1. a. too narrow
   b. main idea
   c. not mentioned
   d. too broad
2–6. Individual answers will vary.

*Any other synonym that makes sense is also acceptable.

Exercise C: Part I

B. 1. challenging
    2. flexible
    3. encounter
    4. alleviate
    5. environment
    6. browse
    7. exaggerate
    8. diverse
    9. cope with
    10. combat

Exercise C: Part II

B. 1. jolt
    2. generate
    3. mature
    4. prosperous
    5. gripe
    6. tend to
    7. perplexing
    8. range
    9. hurdle
    10. hostile

Exercise D*

1. a. rich; wealthy
    b. *Prosperous* indicates success and a good salary. Tourists had to be as wealthy as businesspeople to travel.
    c. not normal; not the usual
    d. because the *average* person is not wealthy
2. a. no
    b. that faraway places are easier to visit now
3. A *host* is a person who receives guests. Here it means that the United States receives foreigners as guests.

4. a. change
    b. *From* shows the original situation; *to* shows what change was made.
5. encounters
6. a. in summary
    b. *In short* introduces a summary of what was explained in lines 15–20.
    c. all the fine points, or subtleties, of the particular culture the student grew up in
7. a. sign
    b. All the characteristics mentioned are signs of culture shock, as indicated by *other signs* in the second sentence. Therefore, *sign* and *symptom* must be synonymous.
8. a. comfortable; relaxed
    b. uncomfortable; nervous
    c. They are opposites.
9. A person who (*-er*) has recently (*new*) arrived (*come*).
10. griping about the problems they've encountered
11. walking around
12. a basic reality
13. Its value is so great that it is uncountable or immeasurable.
14. It introduces a phrase that qualifies as well as emphasizes what came before it.
15. in a foreign country

Exercise E**

1. atypical
2. diverse
3. challenging

---

*Because the wording of individual answers will vary for Exercise D, all logical answers will be considered acceptable.

**Any other synonym that makes sense is also acceptable.

4. hurdles
5. environment
6. perplexing
7. jolt
8. Symptoms
9. hostile
10. mature
11. tends to
12. exaggerate

13. encounters
14. gripes
15. alleviate
16. flexibility
17. cope
18. combating
19. browse
20. priceless

CHAPTER 3

Exercise A
1. F
2. F
3. T
4. T
5. T

Exercise B
1. a. main idea
   b. too broad
   c. too narrow
   d. not mentioned
2–6. Individual answers will vary.

Exercise C: Part I
B. 1. fee
   2. benefit
   3. fulfillment
   4. consequence
   5. burden
   6. compelling
   7. doze off
   8. candidly

Exercise C: Part II
B. 1. phenomenon
   2. significant
   3. void

4. inevitable
5. unsupervised
6. optimum
7. suppress
8. salaried

Exercise D*
1. money
2. the change from full-time mother to working mother
3. a. a later dinner hour
   b. the emotional effects
   c. They are opposites.
   d. It shows a contrast.
   e. conversely
4. a. The second sentence gives examples of the benefits in the first sentence.
   b. advantage; good
5. a. It introduces an explanation of what was presented in the previous sentence.
   b. Because it is not being used in the usual sense: in other words, children simply want to know that their mothers are home, even if they are

*Because the wording of individual answers will vary for Exercise D, all logical answers will be considered acceptable.

not always paying attention to them.

6. a. It introduces the reality of the situation as opposed to what the children would like to be the case.
   b. first concern
7. vary
8. left to do whatever they (the children) want, independently
9. a. stimulated
   b. by the phrase "or stimulated" set off by commas
10. It contrasts the children in paragraph 5, who cope well, with the children in paragraph 6, who have a difficult time coping.
11. a. neglected; left alone
    b. The context of the paragraph gives the idea of being left alone.
    c. It is a family in which the mother does not work and so is home to take care of her children
    d. To show that *around* being used in a special sense: in this context, *around* means "at home."
    e. It introduces a contrasting statement.
12. It introduces an additional fact to support the main idea.
13. spread throughout (our society)
14. assuming and accepting that the situation is real and will not change in the immediate future
15. a. It introduces the list of factors.
    b. availability
    c. The context of the sentence makes it clear: help must be available in the event of an emergency.

Exercise E*
1. constantly
2. compelled
3. salaried
4. fulfillment
5. consequences
6. subtle
7. resentment
8. supervise
9. suppress
10. benefits
11. diverse
12. opportunity
13. perfected
14. conversely
15. void
16. resentful
17. forbid
18. burden
19. doze off
20. optimum
21. candid
22. assistance
23. secure
24. set aside
25. cope

CHAPTER 4

Exercise A
1. F
2. F
3. T

4. T
5. F
6. T

*Any other synonym that makes sense is also acceptable.

Exercise B

1. a. too narrow
   b. main idea
   c. too general
   d. not mentioned
2–6. Individual answers will vary.

Exercise C: Part I

B. 1. priority
   2. receptacle
   3. glance
   4. impact
   5. eliminate
   6. efficient
   7. clutter

Exercise C: Part II

B. 1. disorganized
   2. on time
   3. waste
   4. accumulate
   5. overwhelm
   6. facilitate
   7. appropriate
   8. pressure

Exercise D*

1. put in the wrong place
2. a. usually
   b. The context of the paragraph makes it clear.
3. a. use up completely
   b. The context of the paragraph makes it clear.
4. a. It defines the preceding sentence as cause and the following as result.
   b. disorder
   c. by the phrase "or disorder" set off by commas
5. specific
6. a. The first four examples of staples.
   b. *such as* shows examples being given
   c. a basic food item
   d. It is explained in the following sentence.
   e. available
   f. The context of the two sentences makes it clear: effective planning would keep you from running out of staples.
7. a. rushed; frantic
   b. The context of the sentences makes it clear: mornings are spent rushing around and being late.
8. a. identify
   b. by the phrase "or identify" set off by commas
9. a. in contrast
   b. parts
   c. because the sentence talks about dividing a problem
10. Because it is a subjective term: in other words, not all people consider the same habits as bad habits.
11. a. chores
    b. because the complete tasks we have written down are also defined as "manageable chores"
12. a. get rid of
    b. Because the alternative to *discard* is *put back what you want*.
13. a. that is to say; that is
    b. because the sentence gives two examples of putting similar articles together after *i.e.*

*Because the wording of individual answers will vary for Exercise D, all logical answers will be considered acceptable.

14. by showing that the two actions described are two positive results of equal importance
15. a. at the same time
    b. The following sentence says "exercise while watching TV," and *while* means "at the same time."
16. a. ahead of time
    b. Because the next sentence tells us to prepare for the morning the night before.
17. a. for example
    b. An example follows these words.
18. a. keep
    b. The context of the sentence makes it clear: *keep* is the opposite of *discard*.

Exercise E*
1. cluttered
2. disorganized

3. generally
4. chaos
5. wastes
6. pressure
7. pattern
8. irritating
9. specific
10. out of
11. effectively
12. on time
13. define
14. overwhelming
15. complex
16. segments
17. annoying
18. appointment
19. at once
20. in advance
21. appropriate
22. glance
23. task
24. discard
25. efficient

CHAPTER 5

Exercise A
1. T
2. F
3. F
4. T
5. F
6. F

Exercise B
1. a. too broad
   b. main idea
   c. too narrow
   d. not mentioned
2–6. Individual answers will vary.

Exercise C: Part I
B. 1. profit
   2. substantial
   3. aspect
   4. supplement
   5. expose
   6. vast
   7. detect
   8. defray

Exercise C: Part II
B. 1. verify
   2. inquisitive
   3. insight

*Any other synonym that makes sense is also acceptable.

4. deal with
5. interpret
6. accuracy
7. controversy
8. influential
9. source

Exercise D*

1. a. We have such easy access to news over the world.
   b. very easy to get to
2. a. We can see news on TV, hear it on TV and the radio, and read it in newspapers and magazines.
   b. right away
3. a. journalist
   b. by the phrase "or journalists" set off by commas
4. a. method
   b. by the phrase "or method" set off by commas
5. a. *Media* is the plural form of *medium.*
   b. In line 8, *medium* is used in the singular: "medium, or method." In line 9, the *have* shows *media* is plural: "media *have* become."
6. the passing of time
7. *keep up with; know about (something)* at the time *(it) happens*
8. It shows that what follows is an addition to what precedes.
9. by means of; by way of
10. news items reported by corporations, universities, and government agencies for public information

11. a. because
    b. The second part of the sentence is a result of the first part.
12. a. Both are forms of advertising.
    b. Ads are printed, while commercials are only seen and heard.
13. The most important story of the day, which gets big, dark letters (headlines) on the front, or first, page.
14. It means the stories are actually printed.
15. a. to be the first reporter to get the story to his or her paper to be printed before the other papers get a chance
    b. that is
16. a line stating the name of the reporter who wrote the article
17. the act of making something false or untrue
18. famous people; people making news
19. reporting that requires that one or more reporters spend a period of time getting detailed information by interviewing people, checking reports, following up on events, and so on

Exercise E**

1. instantaneously
2. media
3. advantages
4. detailed
5. lapse
6. abreast of

---

*Because the wording of individual answers will vary for Exercise D, all logical answers will be considered acceptable.
**Any other synonym that makes sense is also acceptable.

7. aspect
8. controversial
9. insight
10. collecting
11. sources
12. supplement
13. profit
14. defray
15. substantial

16. vast
17. inquisitive
18. celebrities
19. rapidity
20. detect
21. accuracy
22. verify
23. goes to press
24. reporters
25. influential

CHAPTER 6

Exercise A
1. T
2. T
3. F
4. F
5. T
6. F

Exercise B
1. a. too broad
   b. main idea
   c. not mentioned
   d. too narrow
2–6. Individual answers will vary.

Exercise C: Part I
B. 1. publicize
   2. jitters
   3. withdrawal
   4. craving
   5. grouchy
   6. surreptitiously
   7. abundant
   8. transition
   9. willpower

Exercise C: Part II
B. 1. hormone
   2. addicted
   3. fatigue
   4. accelerate

5. persevere
6. dose
7. diminish
8. concentrate
9. discipline

Exercise D*
1. To indicate that "tomorrow" is not really meant. It is used to mean "some indefinite time in the future, perhaps never."
2. Because it is not used literally: here it means "end."
3. *Advice* is the noun form of the verb *advise*.
4. a. aspect
   b. from the relationship between the advice and the nouns *health*, *money*, and *cleanliness* (why the advice is sensible)
5. a. shake
   b. by the phrase "or shake" set off by commas
   c. One is thinking constantly about something (such as cigarettes).
6. It introduces a sentence that emphasizes the meaning of the previous sentence.

*Because the wording of individual answers will vary for Exercise D, all logical answers will be considered acceptable.

7. a. act of breathing in
   b. by way of; through
8. cause
9. From the sentence, it is clear that a cycle is a circular pattern in which certain actions are repeated over and over. *Vicious* indicates this pattern is negative or harmful.
10. the last part of the cigarette that is not smoked
11. *Inhalation* is the noun form of the verb *inhale*.
12. a. abrupt cessation, or stopping, of addictive habit
    b. Because *whether . . . or* indicates a choice of two actions: one is *gradual*, so *cold turkey* must be the opposite.
13. a. abrupt
    b. The author advises the shorter of the two methods by recommending cold turkey, so *abrupt* and *cold turkey* must be synonymous.
    c. *Advisable* means something that should be advised; it is an adjective form of *advise*.
    d. because
    e. The first part of the sentence gives a reason on which the second part is based.
    f. and

14. a. because the author isn't using it in a literal sense
    b. that a small period of time is less frightening than an unthinkably long period of time
15. The phrase that follows specifies, or clarifies, what precedes it: *many* means "enough to make you sick."
16. together with

Exercise E*
1. discipline
2. detrimental
3. publicized
4. crave
5. grouchy
6. the jitters
7. addicted
8. inhale
9. accelerates
10. concentrate
11. surreptitiously
12. butts
13. dose
14. quits
15. cold turkey
16. persevere
17. sick
18. transition
19. diminish
20. willpower

CHAPTER 7

Exercise A
1. T
2. T
3. F
4. F
5. T

6. F
7. T

Exercise B
1. a. too broad
   b. too narrow

*Any other synonym that makes sense is also acceptable.

c. not mentioned
d. main idea
2–8. Individual answers will vary.

Exercise C: Part I
B. 1. despicable
2. astute
3. proliferate
4. enterprising
5. abominable
6. contagious
7. alternative
8. deplorable

Exercise C: Part II
B. 1. turnover
2. strata
3. evolve
4. sustain
5. immunity
6. harried
7. suitable
8. mediocre

Exercise D*
1. a. made up of
b. the main salary earner
c. mainly; mostly
d. because it is being set off as a special term or concept
e. the basic unit or core, namely, mother, father, and children
f. It presents the same idea in different terms.
2. a. caused
b. It is a new term.
3. result
4. explains
5. American life
6. gradual change; growth; development

7. a. changed; moved
b. *from* and *to*
8. common; usual
9. a. interfered with; disturbed
b. with regard to
10. a. the people who take care of the children
b. It introduces examples of caretakers.
11. positive and negative feelings together
12. negative effects
13. a. in addition to parents
b. the mixed feelings of the parents
14. a. propose; recommend
b. because the rest of the sentence lists benefits of day-care centers
15. It refers to the benefits of day-care center experiences.
16. easily
17. a. It introduces a contrasting point of view.
b. disagreeing
c. because the rest of the sentence presents a negative point of view toward day-care centers
18. without variation; always. It introduces another detail about poor or mediocre day-care situations.
19. It refers to the frequent turnover in staff members of some day-care centers.
20. the people outside a particular profession or field of expertise
21. always changing
22. become sick with; get
23. those not in favor of
24. a. in fact

*Because the wording of individual answers will vary for Exercise D, all logical answers will be considered acceptable.

b. It introduces a positive reason for exposing children to other children's ailments.

25. a. to those instances in which day-care centers are unacceptable
    b. It shows that what follows emphasizes what precedes it.
    c. give over to with confidence
26. It indicates the extremes in quality of day-care centers.
27. the people who work in the day-care centers
28. physical and mental good health
29. evaluating
30. the relation of one number to another
31. for emphasis
32. a. contrasting ideas
    b. hopeful
33. improve

Exercise E*
1. breadwinner
2. evolved
3. proliferate
4. alternative
5. strata
6. conflicting
7. advocate
8. dissenting
9. mediocre
10. turnover
11. inconsistency
12. contagious
13. despicable
14. Astute
15. assess
16. prolonged
17. suitable
18. upgrading
19. promising
20. dissenters

CHAPTER 8

Exercise A
1. T
2. T
3. F
4. T
5. F
6. F

Exercise B
1. a. too narrow
   b. too broad
   c. not mentioned
   d. main idea
6–9. Individual answers will vary.

Exercise C: Part I
B. 1. emanate from
   2. alter

3. forestall
4. defy
5. boundless
6. cumulative
7. flattering
8. cosmetic
9. ceaseless

Exercise C: Part II
B. 1. tenaciously
   2. sag
   3. wisdom
   4. lucrative
   5. resist
   6. reflect
   7. regulate
   8. secrete

*Any other synonym that makes sense is also acceptable.

Exercise D*

1. a. according to general, per-
      haps mistaken, belief
   b. try very hard
   c. lines in the face
   d. The context of the sentence
      makes it clear.
2. loving being young
3. a. two contrasting ideas
   b. They emphasize two equally
      important ideas about the
      skin.
   c. It provides emphasis.
4. too many to count
5. a. focusing on or concentrating
      on being young
   b. without wrinkles
   c. because smooth skin is with-
      out wrinkles
6. Surgeon is a noun referring to a
   person; surgery refers to the action performed by a surgeon
   and is also a noun.
7. a. the several factors to which
      the aging process of the skin
      is related
   b. heredity
8. a. make smooth or oily
   b. because it is the lubricating
      oil from the glands that
      keeps the skin smooth
   c. secretion; what the gland
      produces
   d. The relative clause defining
      oil glands makes it clear.
9. the eye without the use of any
   instruments such as a telescope
10. It introduces examples of out-
    door sports.
11. according to
12. a. Yes, it does.
    b. *However* introduces a con-
       trasting idea.
13. a. collapse; failure to function;
       the action or result of break-
       ing down
    b. breaking down
    c. because these words are
       used synonymously in the
       sentences
    d. stretched out in time;
       lengthy
    e. The context of the passage
       makes it clear.
14. a. contrasting ideas
    b. continued; growing
    c. by word analysis and the
       context of the sentence
    d. It refers to the fact that the
       program for good skin care
       is just as important for good
       skin care as it is for general
       good health.
15. a diet that has a balance of all
    the foods needed for good
    health

Exercise E**

1. wisdom
2. forestall
3. boundless
4. ceaselessly
5. defying
6. resist
7. lucrative
8. tenacious
9. cosmetic
10. regulates
11. alter
12. secrete
13. lubricates
14. cumulative

---

*Because the wording of individual answers will vary for Exercise D, all logical answers will be
considered acceptable.
**Any other synonym that makes sense is also acceptable.

15. prolonged
16. erosion
17. sag

18. ongoing
19. equally
20. emanate

CHAPTER 9

Exercise A
1. T
2. T
3. F
4. F
5. F

Exercise B
1. a. too narrow
   b. main idea
   c. too broad
   d. not mentioned
2–6. Individual answers will vary.

Exercise C: Part I
B. 1. derive
   2. intensify
   3. enhance
   4. adept
   5. inherent
   6. compassionate
   7. disintegrate

Exercise C: Part II
B. 1. unburden
   2. mutual
   3. vent
   4. therapeutic
   5. plague
   6. turmoil

Exercise D*
1. part
2. the enjoyment of friends' company

3. a. It shows a contrast.
   b. relieve
4. It introduces an additional reason for confiding in friends.
5. a. occasionally
   b. depressed
6. a. teen age
   b. teens
   c. adolescence
   d. old age
   e. the first in a sequence of two
   f. the second in a sequence of two
7. adolescence and old age
8. optimism and an interest in life
9. a. It is being used in a figurative sense.
   b. a group of friends connected to one person
10. a. by custom; traditionally
    b. avoid
    c. not express; keep inside
11. a. people on a middle-income level
    b. people in their forties
12. a. a change from one state to another state
    b. It shows a contrast.
    c. a man whose wife has died
    d. a woman whose husband has died
    e. only
13. a. continuing for a long time
    b. pressure; stress

*Because the wording of individual answers will vary for Exercise D, all logical answers will be considered acceptable.

14. It illustrates, or clarifies, the first sentence.
15. a. It is not used in a literal sense.
    b. to be interesting or exciting
    c. in a similar way
16. a. for example
    b. an instance of people making friends with people who have common interests
17. a. make friends with
    b. development
18. a. under the condition that
    b. It means that both friends receive benefits from the friendship in addition to giving benefits.
19. not honoring a confidence; violating a confidence
20. a. It is not being used in a literal sense.
    b. for life

Exercise E*
1. component
2. intensified
3. plagued
4. compassionate
5. alleviate
6. down in the dumps
7. derive
8. therapeutic
9. adolescence
10. sole
11. unburden
12. adept
13. widows
14. turmoil
15. enhance
16. disintegrates
17. mutual
18. Likewise
19. benefits
20. break

CHAPTER 10

Exercise A
1. F
2. F
3. T
4. F
5. T
6. T
7. T

Exercise B
1. a. main idea
   b. not mentioned
   c. too broad
   d. too narrow
2–7. Individual answers will vary.

Exercise C: Part I
B. 1. ecstatic
   2. encompass
   3. pervade
   4. vigor
   5. version
   6. adhere to
   7. presumably
   8. frequent

Exercise C: Part II
B. 1. innovation
   2. quest
   3. status symbol
   4. emerge

*Any other synonym that makes sense is also acceptable.

5. radical
6. coverage
7. milestone
8. elaborate

Exercise D*

1. created
2. It provides emphasis regarding the duration of time.
3. attacked persistently
4. It is used to emphasize that what follows supports the preceding sentence.
5. an extremely large number
6. for the purpose of being fit, and for no other reason
7. a. It shows they are closely related.
   b. in a very good or optimistic mood
8. An acquaintance is someone you simply know; a friend is someone you know very well.
9. been built; come into being
10. very attractive
11. a. made available
    b. protect
    c. The context of the sentence makes it clear: inhaling smoke is unhealthful.
12. a. habit
    b. sole
13. It introduces facts to support the statement preceding it.
14. a. that companies will save money by giving health club membership to their employees
    b. because at the present time, most companies don't offer this benefit to everyone in their employ
15. It means that mentally and physically, people perform at their highest level.
16. that healthy people live better lives

Exercise E**

1. quest
2. encompasses
3. vigor
4. has pervaded
5. bombard
6. setting aside
7. adhere to
8. innovations
9. exclusively
10. frequent
11. safeguard
12. ecstatic
13. practice
14. status symbol
15. emerging
16. radically
17. Presumably
18. coverage
19. milestone
20. versions

CHAPTER 11

Exercise A
1. T
2. F
3. F
4. T
5. T
6. T

*Because the wording of individual answers will vary for Exercise D, all logical answers will be considered acceptable.
**Any other synonym that makes sense is also acceptable.

Exercise B
1. a. too narrow
   b. too broad
   c. not mentioned
   d. main idea
2–6. Individual answers will vary.

Exercise C: Part I
B. 1. from scratch
   2. brew
   3. irrespective of
   4. assume
   5. convenience food
   6. longevity
   7. concentrated
   8. inedible
   9. investment

Exercise C: Part II
B. 1. pertinent
   2. store
   3. payoff
   4. sound
   5. nomenclature
   6. scrutinize
   7. perishable

Exercise D*
1. a. a very large food store
   b. because they have every kind of food a person might want and other goods besides
2. a. fruit and vegetables that are harvested naturally at the time of year they are made available to consumers
   b. fruit and vegetables that are normally available at other times of the year
3. attractive to the eye
4. appetizing; that make(s) the mouth water

5. They save time and effort.
6. I would think they both contained 100 percent natural juice.
7. It lists five items in order but gives them equal importance.
8. a. nothing more, nothing less
   b. on the other hand
9. It signals to the reader that the second part of the sentence is just as important, if not more so, than the first part.
10. a. that the government issued a law stating that labels must have a list of ingredients
    b. contents of a can or package
11. a. in decreasing order of amount
    b. from the context of the sentences, the second of which explains this term
12. a. recommended daily allowance
    b. It helps the nutrition-conscious consumer eat and prepare a well-balanced diet.
13. It emphasizes the subsequent thought, which expands that of the first sentence.
14. a. nothing; zero
    b. The context of the paragraph suggests this.
15. a. the length of time a product can remain on the store shelves in saleable condition
    b. The rest of the paragraph, which discusses storage and preservation of food, makes the term clear.
16. a. It marks the contrast between the two ideas.
    b. harmless

*Because the wording of individual answers will vary for Exercise D, all logical answers will be considered acceptable.

17. an example
18. a. although
    b. available
    c. The context of the paragraph makes it clear that this information is available on the labels of products.
    d. the information printed on product labels

Exercise E*
1. from scratch
2. convenience foods
3. mouth-watering
4. assume
5. nomenclature

6. ingredients
7. sound
8. longevity
9. deteriorating
10. store
11. innocuous
12. perishable
13. pertinent
14. edible
15. case in point
16. investment
17. scrutinizing
18. payoff
19. Regardless of
20. accessible

CHAPTER 12

Exercise A
1. T
2. F
3. T
4. F
5. T
6. F

8. emanate from
9. peer

Exercise C: Part II
B. 1. resistance
   2. strides
   3. rambunctious
   4. unqualified
   5. solace
   6. uninspired
   7. stabilizing
   8. turbulent
   9. thrive

Exercise B
1. a. main idea
   b. too general
   c. too narrow
   d. not mentioned
2–6. Individual answers will vary.

Exercise C: Part I
B. 1. embedded
   2. promising
   3. count on
   4. assortment
   5. alienation
   6. deter
   7. invariably

Exercise D**
1. a. This is what doctors most often say to patients when they give prescriptions.
   b. It shows that a different idea follows.
2. The semicolon connects two closely related ideas.
3. because *medicine* is not used literally; it is used figuratively

*Any other synonym that makes sense is also acceptable.
**Because the wording of individual answers will vary for Exercise D, all logical answers will be considered acceptable.

literally; it is used figuratively

4. tried out; looked into
5. connection
6. for a long time
7. cause, or make happen
8. It refers to the group of patients having pets.
9. a. for example
   b. heart attack patients without pets
   c. in addition
10. No, not every pet owner enjoys better health and longevity; *in general* indicates that the majority, or most, of them do.
11. Pets are the keys, and the locked doors represent inhibitions, or the inability to express emotions.
12. a. not judging; uncritical
    b. not questioning; totally accepting
13. a. reprimanded
    b. by the phrase "or reprimanded" set off by commas
    c. the dog
14. a. One is a negative action, the other a positive action. In addition, the former is figurative and the second literal.
    b. 1. the tongue-lashing
       2. the dog
       3. It heals hurt feelings.
15. a. stroking
    b. by the phrase "or stroking" set off by commas
    c. What follows after *also* reinforces what follows *not only*.
16. a. to bring back
    b. It is a combination of two words to mean "to play at fighting": the quotation marks show the term is not standard.

17. a. *Holding* simply means having the dog in your arms; *petting* means stroking it.
    b. a relaxing rest
18. It will be helpful to them in the future when they face other responsibilities.
19. very happy; filled with joy
20. a. The second clause is in opposition to the first clause.
    b. They are opposites.
21. a. It provides exercise and an opportunity to start a conversation.
    b. It introduces an additional detail to support the main idea.
    c. It illustrates the term *spontaneous socializing*.
    d. begin
    e. present
    f. It gives a reason in support of the idea in the previous sentence.
22. cannot be compared; the best
23. It usually refers to a person, but here it means the dog.
24. love, warmth, and intimacy
25. a. The doctor usually orders medicine for patients, so now pets are recommended in this manner.
    b. Pet therapy is not a traditional form of medicine.
26. a. It emphasizes the idea of constantly.
    b. It doesn't refer to a specific place.
27. a. since; because (health professionals *are* opening up . . .)
    b. choice

Exercise E*

1. promising
2. link
3. unqualified
4. assortment
5. strides
6. resistance
7. counting on
8. reprimand
9. stabilizing
10. turbulent
11. rambunctious
12. retrieve
13. jubilant
14. solace
15. thrive
16. alienation
17. deter
18. uninspired
19. invariably
20. option

*Any other synonym that makes sense is also acceptable.

Index of Key Words and Phrases

159